PIAF

PIAF

MONIQUE LANGE

TRANSLATED FROM THE FRENCH BY
RICHARD S. WOODWARD

SEAVER BOOKS   NEW YORK

Originally published by Éditions Ramsay, Paris, France,
under the title *Histoire de Piaf.*
Copyright © Éditions Ramsay, Paris, 1979

First Edition 1981
First Printing 1981
ISBN: 0-394-51806-3
Seaver Books ISBN: 0-86579-007-8
Library of Congress Catalog Card Number: 81-4792

LIBRARY OF CONGRESS CATALOGING IN PUBLICATION DATA
Lange, Monique.
[Histoire de Piaf. English]
Piaf.
1. Piaf, Édith, 1915-1963.   2. Singers—France—
Biography.   I. Title.
ML420.P52L33   784.5′0092′4 [B]   81-4792
ISBN 0-394-62428-9   AACR2

Manufactured in the United States of America
Distributed by Grove Press, Inc., New York
SEAVER BOOKS, 333 Central Park West, New York, N.Y. 10025

*The author wishes to thank Andrée Bigard, Simone Margantin. Henri
Contet, Lou Barrier, and the Club of the Friends of Edith Piaf for their
great help in the preparation of this book. Thanks, too, to Gilles Henry,
author of a remarkable genealogy-account of Edith Piaf's life.*

*Finally, special thanks to Jeannette Seaver, whose idea it was for me to
write this book.*

For Carole and Jean

"In this book I have tried to recreate Edith Piaf as she really was: sometimes down and out, other times celebrated and famous. She was both generous and cruel, dramatic and funny. I sought out those who knew her and gathered letters, photographs, and unpublished documents that cast light on the hidden face of the myth: the real Piaf who burnt herself out mercilessly and totally, and in so doing touched the hearts of millions. She, who could devour some, was also capable of giving her all to her adoring public."

—MONIQUE LANGE

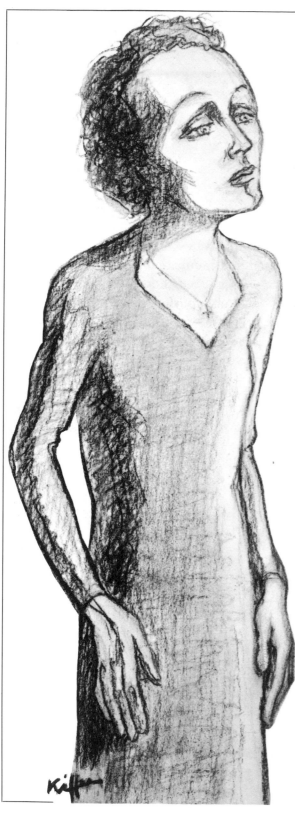

CONTENTS

Edith Piaf's family traced its roots back to Normandy, and in particular to the little village of Castillon, 34 km from Caen, 11 from Bayeux (home of the famous Bayeux tapestry), and 4 from Balleroy.

Piaf of course was Edith's stage name. Her real name, Gassion, according to Dauzat's *Etymological Dictionary*, was a diminutive form of Gassie (in its older form, Garsia). In the region of Béarn in the 14th century the name occurs under the alternate spelling of Gassio, probably an alternate spelling of the Spanish name Garcia.

Edith's first known ancestor was a Richard Gassion, born ca. 1656. He married Marie Douétil sometime prior to 1677, when their first child Jean (or Joan, as it was sometimes spelled) was born. Richard was a farm laborer, living in the hamlet of Bois, near Castillon, where he died on December 12, 1716. The family moved to Falaise about 100 years later.

1
CHILDHOOD

She spent her whole life
taking revenge on her
frightful youth.
—Bruno Coquatrix

Her "sister" Momone was
the constant reminder of
their monstrous childhood.
—Henri Contet

CALVADOS

Today, almost two decades after her death, the voice of Edith Piaf is still with us—a voice that wells up from the depths of night to carry us into her own nocturnal world, a world she fashioned, through pain and sorrow, from her poverty, her childhood, and her endless succession of tragic love affairs.

A thousand years from now Piaf's voice will still be heard, and each time we hear it we will wonder anew at its strength, its violence, its lyrical magic. Where, in God's name, did such a voice come from?

The fact is, it came from a long way away, from the mountains of Kabylia. Edith's grandmother was Moroccan and, performing under the name Aicha, had a trained-flea act with a traveling circus.

That voice also came from ignorance, fear, and a terrible lack of affection. It came from the memory of Hell.

Edith liked to say that she was descended from a Marshal of the Empire from Pau, a town in southwestern France at the foot of the Pyrénées. There are in fact Gassions in Pau, but Edith's paternal ancestors, as far back as anyone can trace them, came from Normandy, from the village of Castillon, which, when Richard Gassion was born there in 1656, numbered 331 souls. Richard Gassion was a farm laborer, and the records show that the family remained there for a hundred years or so, at which time they moved to Falaise, where they worked in the hosiery trade.

It was Edith's grandfather, Victor Alphonse Gassion, who brought show business into the family. Born on December 10, 1850, at Falaise, Victor Alphonse joined the Ciotti Circus and traveled with it throughout

12

France and Europe. A horse lover, he ended up a groom. He met his wife—one of twenty-two children—at her father's inn, at Carvin in the Pas-de-Calais. She was ten years younger than he, and following family tradition, Louise Léontine Descamps gave Victor Alphonse fourteen children, born in the course of their peripatetic career with the Ciotti Circus. Edith's father was one of the eldest—Louis Alphonse Gassion, born on May 10, 1881.

All the men in the family were short. The tallest was only five feet four; Edith's father stood only four feet ten inches, which was to be exactly her height as well.

Louis Gassion spent the first ten years of his life in Falaise, then he too joined the Ciotti Circus. There he became the mountebank that Edith always loved.

> Louis Alphonse Gassion
> Step right up, folks!
> See him walk on his hands!
> The upside-down man,
> The man who can twist himself
> into a thousand shapes:
> The human pretzel man!

He was a slight, good-looking man—he weighed less than a hundred pounds—when he met Anetta Maillard at the Paris Fair. She was selling nougat candy and operating a merry-go-round. And since neither of these jobs brought in much, she sang as well. Louis Alphonse seduced

Edith's paternal grandfather, Victor-Alphonse Gassion, was an inveterate horseman. He was born in Falaise on December 10, 1850, and spent most of his working life with the circus, as a groom. In this early photograph, he is shown performing on his favorite horse.

13

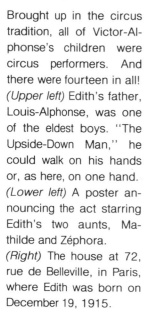

Brought up in the circus tradition, all of Victor-Alphonse's children were circus performers. And there were fourteen in all! *(Upper left)* Edith's father, Louis-Alphonse, was one of the eldest boys. "The Upside-Down Man," he could walk on his hands or, as here, on one hand. *(Lower left)* A poster announcing the act starring Edith's two aunts, Mathilde and Zéphora. *(Right)* The house at 72, rue de Belleville, in Paris, where Edith was born on December 19, 1915.

her without too much trouble, and they were married in 1914. Louis was then thirty-three, Anetta sixteen. As dowry, she brought him that amazing voice—the only present her daughter would ever receive from her.

A few months before the outbreak of World War I, they had a little girl. History doesn't tell whether she was conceived at 72 rue de Belleville, but there, in any case, was where Anetta went into labor. What we do know for sure is that Louis Gassion, who was as much given to drink as he was to womanizing, set off when the labor pains began in search of an ambulance. But along the way he stopped off at every bar and bistro between the rue de Belleville and the hospital. So it was that Anetta gave birth not on the pavement of the rue de Belleville, as legend has it, but on a policeman's cape in the hallway of their house.

In biographies of Edith Piaf, you very often find not one but several truths, several versions of the same event. The reason is twofold: first, her life has already become a legend, told and retold in serials, comic strips,

14

photo romances, and books; and second, because Edith often preferred not to tell the truth, or simply didn't know it.

Let's see if we can come closer to *her* truth. The child who came into the world at five in the morning that day, up above the rue de Belleville, was a scrawny creature, already suffering from rickets: a child born into abject poverty.

A nurse who lived a block or so away, at 4 rue de la Chine, cut—"in the absence of the father"—the umbilical cord of the little girl, who was named Edith, in honor of Edith Cavell, an English nurse who a few days earlier had been shot by the Germans. Just because a man is a drunk doesn't mean he can't be patriotic.

The war was on. Louis Gassion was called up to serve his country. To try and keep body and soul together, Anetta went up to the Buttes de Montmartre to sing her sad songs in the cheap music halls and cafés where, at the same time, the future great of French stage and screen, Michel Simon, was performing his acrobatic dances. Soon Anetta aban-

Edith's father, like most men of his age, was called up into army service, for World War I was raging. When he came home on leave in 1917, he found that his wife Anetta had been too poor to care for the child, and had turned little Edith over to her maternal grandmother.

15

(Above . left) A picture taken in the garden at Bernay of Edith's grandfather, Victor-Alphonse, the year of his death. Seventy-seven at the time, as a result of his profession he had suffered from a profusion of falls and broken bones, and at the end he was virtually paralyzed. To his left, seated, is his wife Louise, also known as ''Maman Titine.'' Behind him, on the left, is one of ''Maman Titine's'' sisters, and standing is their daughter Zéphora. Seated in the center, clutching the Teddy Bear, is Zéphora's daughter Mauricette.

(Above right) Edith's mother. Also a singer, she died in 1945.

doned little Edith to her Moroccan grandmother, who lived in a slum building on the rue Rébeval.

Edith's grandmother was not a bad woman, but despite her origins she followed neither the basic tenets of hygiene nor of the Koran: she laced the water in the child's bottle with red wine—under the pretext that it killed germs—and almost never bathed her.

Line Marsa—that was the stage name that Edith's mother assumed—died one night in August 1945, of an overdose of morphine. The young addict she was living with panicked and carried her down into the street.

16

So she died, literally, in the gutter, just as Louis Gassion had predicted she would. The news of her mother's death was kept from Edith as long as possible. Edith had a morbid fear of drugs, yet near the end of her life, ironically, she too succumbed to them.

If she never forgave her mother for having abandoned her as a child, she never blamed her or complained about the poverty that had molded her. "I wouldn't be Piaf if I hadn't lived through all that," she used to say.

Edith was in such frightful shape when Papa Gassion came home on leave in 1917 that he could scarcely believe that scrawny, scab-ridden infant could be his. He spirited her away from his mother-in-law and took her out to Bernay, in Normandy, to live with his mother, who since her husband's death ran "a house of a rather special sort" there.

The arrival of little Edith and the "brave soldier home from the war" was cause for great rejoicing. The ladies of the establishment were beside themselves. Many of them were in the profession in order to provide for their own children, who at birth had to be sent to live with a wet-nurse, and so they coddled and pampered Edith as though she were their own.

From the poverty of Montmartre to the green abundance of Normandy in one fell swoop! Her eight adoring mothers taught her to curtsy and mind her manners. "It's only proper: the people who come to visit are the finest gentlemen in town."

A photograph of Edith taken at this time, after two years of coddling by her multiple mothers, reveals a ravishing little girl with radiant eyes, ringlets, and a bow in her hair. She is flanked in the photograph by two of her cousins, neither as pretty as she. She would pick out tunes on the piano in the living room, and crawl up on the knees of the gentlemen visitors. She was a happy child.

One lovely spring morning, Edith suddenly became blind. Actually, she had an inflammation of the cornea, or keratitis, which cures itself in time. But the ladies of the house would never believe that her miraculous cure, on August 21, 1921, was not the direct result of their fervent prayers. As thanks, they closed the house the following Sunday to go and render homage to the little nun, Thérèse of Lisieux, who would remain Edith's favorite saint till the end of her life.

The child was now six years old.

That "miracle" remains one of the favorite themes of the Piaf legend.

Since she could now see again, she would have to go to school. They would have to buy her those blue graph-paper notebooks that children used and that Edith would adore for the rest of her life. The parish priest told Madame Louise that he would like to have a word with Edith's

Edith, center, in 1917 or 1918, at her grandmother's house in Normandy, with two unidentified little cousins. After her husband's death, "Madame Louise" opened a house of a special kind. The years Edith spent here she would remember as "very happy" ones.

father. When Louis Gassion arrived, the priest delivered a short but simple sermon: now that little Edith could see again—and it was indeed a miracle—it was not proper that her newly opened eyes should gaze upon Sin. In other words, she should leave her grandmother's house of dubious repute forthwith.

Edith's father took her under his wing again, but this time it was to join him in his bohemian existence. She was not yet seven when her vagabond life with her father began.

They traveled from town to town. Edith's father would spread out a carpet on the sidewalk and perform a few simple tricks. Edith would pass the hat.

When they had earned enough money to have some left over after they had eaten, they would go to a hotel; otherwise they slept wherever they could. Whenever they remained in one place for more than a day or

18

two, Edith's father, whose heart was in the right place, would send her to school. She loved to learn, and would clutch her notebooks to her heart.

They had a little monkey with them. It was Edith's job to take care of it. She didn't like the monkey. If she didn't look after it properly, her father would thrash her. He may have had a good heart, but he also had a quick hand.

On special feast days, Edith was in charge of cooking the lamb stew. She would climb up on a chair, since she was too short, kneel down on the stove next to the stew, and stir it with a wooden stick.

Piaf, claims the actress Marie Bell, would wash the lamb before cooking it. She also washed steaks and veal. The habit must date from that period of her life. One can't help thinking of the maggots in the meat in the film *Battleship Potemkin.*

Among the acts that Edith's father performed on the sidewalk was the

A street scene in Belleville. When she was an infant, Edith used to play in these streets, with little girls such as those pictured.

Edith Gassion, a little girl
in a sailor suit.

talking table. Edith would hide underneath the table, which was covered with a cloth or rug. Then she would answer her father's questions with little knocks: Tap! Tap! Tap! That was the talking table act.

One day, to Edith's great embarrassment, her father, slightly in his cups, let the cloth fall off the table, revealing to the good-natured crowd a little girl in rags crouched there on all fours.

Papa Gassion resorted to the same kind of method to teach Edith her French history. He would fire questions at her point-blank:

"Who devastated the city of Soissons, and by what means?"

"Who was it who said, 'Rally round my white feather'?"

"Who was responsible for making chicken the traditional Sunday dish?"

Each time she didn't know the answer, she received a slap across the face. This rather special teaching method instilled in her a love of history—and of getting smacked. And, as when the imminence of death is upon us we revert to our childhood, so Edith, during the last days of her life, read and reread, with a consuming passion, the history of France.

Edith's father loved women as much as he loved drink, and in his peregrinations had more than one trick up his sleeve.

As he performed, walking on his hands, his head upside-down, he would spot the women in the crowd he liked, and once back on his feet he would steer Edith to them, telling her to do her "little girl without a mama" number as she passed the hat. She was eight years old, and was getting her first lessons in acting.

"Why do you look so sad, child?" they would ask.

"Because I don't have a mommy."

"You don't have a mother?" The woman would sigh, her heart melting.

"No," Edith would respond, gazing up with her big blue eyes.

"Where is your mother?"

"She left me," the child would answer. "Would you like to be my mother?"

Not a woman in the world could resist her. In fact, that would be the story of Edith's life: no one ever had the strength to resist her. She was magnetic.

The potential mother would hurry over to the hotel the next day to tuck the little girl in. Daddy Gassion would pay her a compliment or two, and as soon as he had her properly warmed up, Edith would be sent out into the hallway to stand guard.

Sometimes things worked out even more simply: all three of them would sleep together in the little iron bed.

The cinema at Bernay has been renamed the *Piaf*.

The only song Edith knew, when she first went out into the streets, singing to earn her bread, was the *Marseillaise*.

2
THE VOICE

For me, singing is a way of escaping. It's another world. I'm no longer on earth.

—Edith Piaf

In the song *The Voyage of the Poor Black,* if at the end of the song I move my arms as though I'm swimming, it's because when I sang it for the first time I wasn't very sure of the words, and so I began to move my arms that way to cover it up.

—Edith Piaf

Every time she sings you have the feeling she's wrenching her soul from her body for the last time.

—Jean Cocteau

I'm sure that a good performer could read Baudelaire to a music-hall audience and pull it off.

—Edith Piaf

We knew that her voice, so filled with distress, so full of torment, was really a voice of love.

—Jean Noli

Edith sang. And this tiny creature, so miserable and scrawny—so wounded and shattered by life, so guilty and yet so innocent of her sins and misfortunes—this little creature knocked us out. . . . That voice, which betrayed her worries and revealed the depths of her solitude, ultimately made her sincere. That voice made us love her. For there's no point denying it: we did love her.

—Jean Noli

(Above) A photo of Edith dedicated by her to Camille Ribon, a man with whom she used to sing in the army barracks.

(Right) She also used to sing in the streets of Pigalle.

One winter colder than most, Papa Gassion fell ill. There wasn't a penny left in the house; in fact, there wasn't any house. Edith, not yet ten, went out into the street. Since begging wasn't her style, she sang the only song she knew by heart: the *Marseillaise*. She collected more money than she ever had when she passed the hat for her father. La Môme, the "kid", was born. An extraordinary kid whose voice would take the world by storm.

Piaf discovered her voice that day the same way that adolescents wake up one day and discover their good looks, their power of seduction. She also discovered the heady feelings of freedom, rebellion, and independence, which she clung to as long as she lived.

Piaf was of the same mold as Victor Hugo's Gavroche and the children in Chaplin's films. She was the little girl in *Modern Times*—the one who had to steal if she wanted to eat, and jump out the window if she wanted to get away from the cops. Like Gavroche, she had the street smarts and daring of kids who have known utter poverty, the guts of street urchins, of shoe-shine boys, of the Arab beggars no higher than your knees. These children were always hanging around Piaf, in the pockets of her black dress, as it were, like Tom Thumb's pebbles.

24

Montmartre, in the 1930s.

We don't really know very much about these early years. Edith never talked about them. Father and daughter would often sleep outdoors, under the stars, and when Edith was too cold her father would warm her with a swig or two of brandy.

When she was fifteen, Edith left her father to strike out on her own. And she made it. . . . She didn't always have enough to eat, but, drunk with freedom, she would wander through the Paris streets, singing for her supper . . . and her lunch and breakfast too. Tagging along was her faithful friend Momone, whom Piaf called her "sister," and who in later years actually tried to pass herself off as Piaf's real sister.

Edith's method was to sing in the courtyards. Momone would pass the

26

hat, just as Edith had done for many years for her father. They slept in cellars, where one or the other would have to stay awake throughout the night, armed with a fat stick to chase the intruding rats away. It was because of these lower depths they had shared that Edith always forgave Momone, no matter what she did, in their later years.

"My life when I was a kid might strike you as awful, but actually it was beautiful. I lived in Barbès, in Pigalle, in Clichy, in the chic sections of town, in the theater districts, the streets where the whores hung out. I was hungry, I was cold. But I was also free . . . free not to get up in the morning, not to go to bed at night, free to get drunk if I liked, to dream . . . to hope."

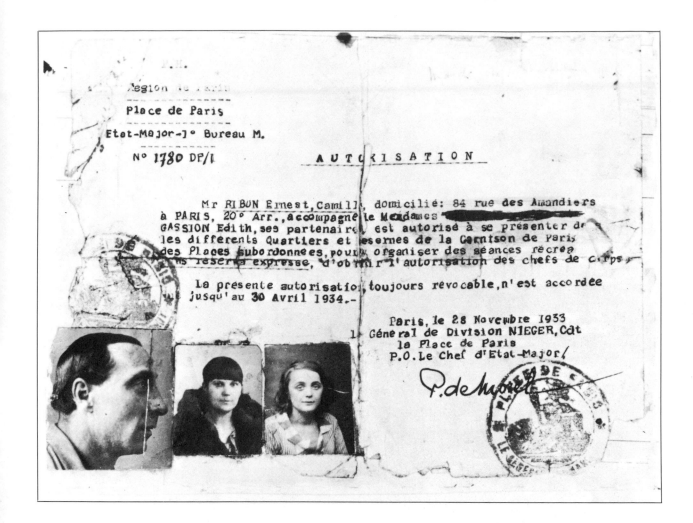

M.H.

Region de Paris

Place de Paris

Etat-Major-1° Bureau M.

N° 1780 DP/I   A U T O R I S A T I O N

Mr RIBON Ernest,Camill, domicilié: 84 rue des Amandiers
à PARIS, 20° Arr.,accompagné le Mesdames ▬▬▬▬▬▬
GASSION Edith,ses partenaire, est autorisé à se présenter de
les differents Quartiers et casernes de la Garnison de Paris
des Places subordonnees,pour organiser des séances recréa
tions reserve expresse, d'obtenir l'autorisation des chefs de corps

La présente autorisation toujours révocable,n'est accordée
que jusqu'au 30 Avril 1934.-

                              Paris, le 28 Novembre 1933
                              l. Général de Division NIEGER,Cdt
                              la Place de Paris
                              P.O.Le Chef d'Etat-Major/

Authorization by the military authorities for Edith to sing in the army barracks to entertain the soldiers.

One of Edith's first big hits occurred while she was still singing in the streets. The song was called *The Devil's Fiancée,* a hit tune at the time. She was singing one day in 1932 in the Faubourg Saint-Martin, a relatively poor section of Paris, and attracted a huge crowd. In those days it wasn't unusual, or against the law, for big crowds to gather to listen to street kids sing. In any case, that day the police had to be called and Edith was fined. The police lieutenant in charge refused to let her go unless she sang *I've Got the Blues,* another hit of the day. If she didn't, he warned, she'd spend the night at the station-house. It wouldn't be the first time, Edith must have thought. Anyway, she obliged, and when Momone had made her rounds she found her old Basque beret was bulging with coins—five pounds' worth when they weighed it!

That night, Edith had the inkling—naïve no doubt and vague, but nonetheless intense—that one day her voice would reach out and conquer the world. It would be her response to her mother's having abandoned her.

The parameters of Edith's world in these days were from Pigalle to Ménilmontant, where she became fascinated by pimps, hoods, and Paris toughs.

"I've always wanted to sing, just as I've always known that one day I would have my own niche in the annals of song. It was a feeling I had simply from hearing the crowd's response to my songs."

When he wasn't too busy drinking, Edith's father would make some half-hearted efforts to find his daughter who, when she didn't make enough singing in the streets and courtyards of Paris, would also sing in the barracks with Old Man Ribon.

Until her dying day, Edith always helped Old Man Ribon. She helped him just as she helped thousands of others. Unfortunately for him, Edith died before he did, a full decade in fact: Old Ribon died in 1973, in a miserable garret in the heart of Montmartre, a rat-infested place he had lived in and refused to leave—the same sort of rats that had kept Edith awake at night when she was little.

In the barracks, Edith began to forge her "myth of the ideal man": the handsome soldier with limpid eyes.

> *He had a scar*
> *That ran diagonally*
> *From brow to chin,*
> *Black hair, light eyes,*
> *His skin burnt by the sun . . .*[1]

Yet it was in the arms of Little Louis, an insolent delivery boy who outstared her one day when she was singing at the Porte des Lilas, that she first knew real love. They set up housekeeping together, in a mangy hotel on the rue de Belleville. They paid thirty francs a week for the room, and on Sundays they would take in a film at the Alcazar, on the rue du Jourdain. Little Louis would pay for Edith's two-franc seat. It was at the Alcazar that she discovered Charlie Chaplin, his various characters, as well as Tom Mix and Rudolph Valentino.

Edith was pregnant. Little Louis didn't want her to sing in the streets anymore. But she was incapable of holding a steady job. After three days in a dairy shop, she ran away. "I couldn't help it. I can't stand the smell of cheese!"

Little Louis set up his household by stealing. Not much, just a few little things now and then. Edith cooked over their meager stove, usually some kidney beans heated up right in the can.

If Little Louis was the first man that Edith hurt, he was not destined to be the last. She left him for her mythical *Amant de la Coloniale.* She went

---

[1] From *Mon amant de la Coloniale,* 1936. The original text for this and all the other songs in this book appears at the back in the section entitled *Songs in French.*

back to singing in the courtyards, with Momone at her side and holding her baby, Cécelle, in her arms. She didn't bring her baby along to melt the hearts of her listeners, but in order not to leave the child behind as her mother had left her. But she had no idea how to take care of the baby. How could she have known how to raise a child, she who had never been raised herself?

Little Cécelle died of meningitis at the Tenon Hospital. She died, above all, because of Edith's own miserable childhood, and because of her ignorance. It was August 1935. The baby was not yet two.

Part of the Piaf legend fits in here: the story of how she didn't have the money to pay for her daughter's burial. Everyone in Pigalle, Belleville, and Ménilmontant adored her, and chipped in as much as they could. The problem was they were just as poor as Edith. She took a man up to her room for ten francs.

Years later, when she was famous, Edith decided that it would be more seemly to relate that, indeed, she had taken him up to her room, but that

Testimonial from Colonel Robert de Saint Vincent, Commander of the 72nd Artillery Regiment, about the evening's performance by Edith and her colleagues, just before Christmas, 1933: "An interesting and varied evening, where the performers were talented and showed great zest, despite the small audience."

31

Paris in 1934

he had never touched her. When they got to the room, Edith burst into tears. "What's the matter?" the man asked. "I'm doing this so I can pay for my daughter's funeral," sobbed Edith. The man gave her the money without asking for anything in return. RUN ALONG, KID, AND CHEER UP. LIFE ISN'T EASY, IS IT? screamed a French headline when it told the story. "A real gentleman," Edith sighed, fifteen years after the event.

After her break with Little Louis and the baby's death, Edith hung around Pigalle and Ménilmontant, and became fascinated by rather unsavory men. Three men weren't enough to blot out the memory of Cécelle. She drank, she laughed, she raised hell. Her mother had abandoned her; she hadn't abandoned *her* baby: it was Cécelle who had left her.

She ran into some pimps. She was mesmerized by them. She sang for them, but she was very young and it was they who would make her sing. She was a force of nature. She wouldn't become a prostitute, as her mother suggested one night when their paths crossed up in Montmartre, but she was obliged to fork over thirty francs a day to Albert, the handsomest of the three pimps. She paid him out of what she earned singing. Rosita, the other woman, paid out of what she made whoring on the rue Blanche.

Even though she wasn't a prostitute, she had to abide by the laws of the underworld, which were ruthless. While singing in the dance halls, she would keep an eye out for the women wearing jewels, and that evening, at the Nouvelle Athènes, she would point them out to Albert.

Albert would make conversation with the ladies, flatter them and flirt with them, then clean them out in the nearest alley. With the money from the stolen jewelry, Albert would take Edith and his buddies out for a wild night on the town.

When the party was over, Edith would sing to them:

> *The swells, the blasé, the depraved,*
> *with their broads who stare at us dewey-eyed*
> *come up here slumming*
> *and drink our red wine.*
> *. . . We feel their flesh quivering in our arms,*
> *while we hold them tight and whisper:*
> *We're the real hoods, the roughs,*
> *the hooligans, we're the Paris toughs . . .*[2]

Edith loved the night. She would always love it. She was afraid of the day.

She used to walk from Pigalle to the Champs-Elysées. She sang in the cinemas and the local dance halls, but what she still loved best was to sing in the streets. She loved the pavement the way some people love flowers or the sea. Paris clung to her body. It was Paris that coursed through her veins.

Not only Paris: the Paris toughs as well. When she sang she gave them goose pimples, she made shivers run up and down their spines, she made their hearts beat faster. But then, immediately afterward, she made sure she would be brutally rejected: by her embarrassing gestures, that feverishness, that eagerness, that reckless generosity that was part and parcel of her being. She would always chase after men who didn't want any part of her. Edith *was* the words of her songs—all the words—and all the melodrama too. She was everything that rejected her.

> *Alas, one night my heart was broken,*
> *My lover did not come back . . .*[3]

She was adored and she was scorned. Even Raymond Asso, who was her first real teacher and who did love her, Asso-the-Jealous, who beat her (which she loved), even he could see that Pigalle adored her.

Edith almost always sang on the Right Bank.

She never crossed the Seine.

Why?

The man who discovered Piaf was Louis Leplée, who owned a nightclub, Gernys, and had earlier been a nightclub performer himself. He was the nephew of the famous Polin, a nightclub comic at the end of the 19th century. Poets advertised his talents at the time with these lines:

If it's laughter
You're after,
Go and hear
The man Polin.
He'll stand you on your
ear.

Other famous nightclub artists of his era were Mayol, Dranem, and the unforgettable Mistinguett.

3

LEPLÉE

Leplée met a spahi one night in Pigalle. He invited the handsome soldier, all decked out in his spanking colonial uniform, to come to Gernys the next night. Leplée was there with Piaf, very late; most of the guests had left. "Boy, is that kid handsome," Piaf told Leplée. "Wait a minute," he said, "he's not for you. He's mine." At which point Leplée moved to the attack. "Hey, fellow," the spahi said when he understood, "you've got me all wrong. I'm not that kind." Leplée told Edith how disappointed he was. "I'm really sorry it didn't work out," she said, "but since it didn't, you won't mind, will you?" With which she hailed a taxi, and off Edith and the soldier went.

—*Détective* magazine

There was a true mafia around the owner of Gernys, which I suspect was capable of anything in the book—and probably several that weren't. —Philippe Hériat

A young homosexual who went under the name of The Panther in the gay underworld, had divested Leplée of his wallet after having threatened him with a gun in a hotel just around the corner from the flower market at the Madeleine.

—*Détective* magazine

Louis Leplée.

One sunny September afternoon, Edith was singing at the corner of the rue Troyon and the Avenue MacMahon, in one of the poshest sections of Paris.

The beak open like a sparrow
The bold eye of a sparrow
Singing of love like two sparrows.[4]

A well-dressed man listened to her sing, a frown on his face. Edith became aware of him, of his gaze both tender and sad. After her song, he came over to her.

"Are you out of your mind? You're going to ruin your voice."

"A girl has to eat, doesn't she?"

"Of course you do, child, but you can earn your daily bread another

36

way. With that voice, why don't you sing in a cabaret?"

"You have a contract for me to sign?"

"Come and see me Monday afternoon at four o'clock, at Gernys. You can sing me your whole repertoire, and we'll see what we can do with you."

The man scribbled his name and address in the margin of the newspaper he was carrying, and handed Edith a five-franc note.

"My name is Louis Leplée and I run Gernys."

Edith didn't know it, but she had just been reborn. Monday afternoon, she was still lounging in bed in her tiny room on the rue Orfila, in Ménilmontant, when something stronger than she, some unknown force, made her jump out of bed.

She dashed downstairs, ran to the Métro, and arrived at Gernys an hour late.

"An hour late! Just think what we have to look forward to when you become a star!"

Edith sang her entire repertoire, which ranged from Damia to Tino Rossi. When she proposed singing an aria from *Faust*, Leplée drew the line.

The fact was, he had heard enough, and was bowled over by Edith's singing. He may have been well on in years, an aging homosexual who was pretty much of a loner, but he knew genius when he heard it—it didn't happen all that often—and this little girl from Belleville and Ménilmontant certainly had it.

He hired her on the spot, and told her she would start that Friday. Meanwhile, he wanted her to add four songs to her repertoire, four songs that suited her to a T: *Les Mômes de la cloche, Nini peau de chien, La Valse brune,* and *Je me sens dans tes bras, si petite.*

"What's your name?" Leplée asked her.

"Edith Gassion."

"That won't do for a stage name."

"I'm also known as Tania, Denise Jay, and Huguette Elia." They were the names she used when she sang in music halls.

"Can't say any of them is all that much better," Leplée sighed. "Let me see . . . you're a real Paris sparrow, a *moineau,* and Kid Sparrow would be great for you. But unfortunately there's already a singer, Môme Moineau, so that's out. What's the slang for *moineau?* Piaf, that's it. You're a slang kid anyway. Piaf. We'll name you Kid Piaf!"

That Friday, Piaf, who had brought tears to the eyes of the poor and downtrodden of Paris, who had sent chills up the spines of soldiers and sailors, had the same astonishing effect on the wealthy. As they sipped their champagne and ate their *Coq du Chanturges* at Gernys, they heard

The year is 1931, and one of the most popular amusements of the time was the apache ball. Pictured here are guests at one organized by Francis Carco.

tell of a poverty and misery of which they had never had even the faintest notion. In 1935, Belleville and Ménilmontant were not just a few miles away from the Champs-Elysées, they were a world apart. Edith was an apparition, fervent and burning.

Leplée introduced her himself:

Ladies and gentlemen, a few days ago I was strolling along the rue Troyon. A little girl was singing on the sidewalk. A little girl whose face was pale and full of sadness. I can't tell you what her voice did to me. I was moved, more than I can tell you. Overwhelmed. I wanted to share this girl, this Paris child, with you. She doesn't own an evening dress, and if she knows how to take a bow, it's because I taught her how yesterday. She's going to appear here tonight just as I first saw her on the street that day: without any makeup, no stockings, in a plain cheap little skirt. And so here she is, ladies and gentlemen, Kid Piaf!

When she came out to perform, Edith had thrown around her shoulders the shawl that was covering the piano. But when she raised her arms over her head as she sang, Joseph Kessel, Maurice Chevalier, Mistinguett, Fernandel and the other guests could see that the sweater she was wearing had only one sleeve. She hadn't had time to knit the other one! But that didn't keep her from scoring a triumph.

"She's got it, that kid has," Maurice Chevalier exulted. "A real talent!"

Leplée was a strange but somehow touching person. His uncle Polin had been a cabaret star a generation earlier, so he too was a showbusiness child.

In his younger days he himself had had a successful career as a singer in the cabaret world. Wounded in World War I, he walked with a pronounced limp. He had first opened a small cabaret up in Montmartre in the cellars of the Palace, on the rue du Faubourg Montmartre. The backer of that venture, a man named Dufresne, also a homosexual, had

Piaf seated on Leplée's lap.

39

Mistinguett.

been murdered. Leplée later opened a transvestite cabaret in Pigalle, Libertys, where he performed while his co-owner greeted the clientele in drag. But Libertys' management was in no way prejudiced, and women were not only welcome but used to sing there songs so bawdy they would make a guardsman blush. That was in 1932.

From there Louis Leplée moved on to more elegant things. The formula for Gernys was innovative: it was a restaurant that opened only at nine in the evening, with entertainment until four in the morning.

Edith the night-owl and Louis Leplée were made for each other. All her life she had trouble going to bed before dawn. Piaf's success was immediate, and she proved that she could bring tears to the eyes of the swells, too. But to Leplée's great annoyance and despair, as soon as her act was over, Edith, instead of mingling with the customers, headed back for Pigalle where all her old buddies were waiting for her at La Belle Ferronière. There she blew her money with, and on, her Pigalle friends, as she would blow it the rest of her life.

Actually, Leplée was deeply touched by Edith. He took her in hand. She was a gift Providence had given him to lighten his later years. He wanted to teach her how to live. He loved her. She called him Papa, not because she had for a moment denied her own acrobat-drunk father, but because she sensed that Leplée, like her, was also a loner, someone society treated as an outcast. Though they had arrived at their success by very different routes, both Louis and Edith were outsiders.

Louis Leplée was proud—he had introduced so many night-club artists to the rich and famous of Paris—to have discovered this youngster, this little sparrow fallen from a nest she never really had, and he was sure she was bound for glory. Still, though Edith could be influenced, ultimately she remained unregenerate, fiercely and totally independent, and she never changed. There were times when Leplée had to lock Edith in her dressing room to keep her from slipping back down into the street to sing when she had blown all her money and needed a franc or two to pay for a movie.

The truth was—and Leplée was well aware of it—that though Edith might have been impressed and dazzled when someone pointed out to her the French political leader Philippe Hériat in the audience, or the son of King Fouad I, Prince Farouk, or Jean Tranchant; though she couldn't believe her eyes when Mermoz invited her to have a glass of champagne with him at his table after her act, and then proceeded to buy her the whole basket of flowers that the vendor was selling, it was in the streets that Edith felt most at home, and it was her street audience she loved the most. It was that audience she was looking for all her life, as it was looking for her, an audience she both scorned and adored. A year before her death she murmured, as she collapsed on stage: "I can't do this to my

The writer Joseph Kessel, who, thirty years later, introduced Edith, from atop the Eiffel Tower.

Among the glittering crowd also present that first night at Leplée's were Jean Mermoz (pictured here), the famous aviator who in 1930 had been the first to fly from France to South America and who, that night, bought the entire contents of the flower vendor's basket and gave them to Piaf.

public!" Her public was the only lover who didn't let her down, because it was the only one who hadn't defiled her.

At Leplée's Edith met a man named Jacques Bourgeat one night, and it would turn out to be one of the most important encounters of her life.

Jacques Bourgeat was a self-taught poet, a man of humble origins who had little formal education. At the age of twelve, he was already an electrician on the Paris trolley lines. But he aspired to higher things; he lusted after knowledge, and wrote poems. Later he discovered the public library, and in his cheap second-hand copy of the Larousse dictionary he listed the titles of all the books he wanted to read. On Sundays—because it was free that day—he visited the Louvre, exploring its every floor and wing from top to bottom.

Edith had only been at Leplée's for three days when, as chance would

Piaf, dressed fit to kill, one Sunday in the mid-30s on the Place du Tertre.

have it, a wealthy friend of Bourgeat's invited Jacques to come and hear her. When Edith came out and began to sing, he couldn't believe his eyes or ears. After her number, Jacques' friend invited her over to have a glass of champagne with them. And there began one of the most beautiful and touching friendships imaginable. It wasn't one that Edith would sing about: she simply lived it. The tenderness between them is little known, because they managed to keep it out of the public eye, but it was certainly one of the most touching aspects of Edith's life.

"They tell me you're a poet," Edith said to Bourgeat that night at Gernys. "In that case, why don't you write me some songs? I live at the Piccadilly Hotel in the rue Pigalle. Come by and see me tomorrow."

The next afternoon, Bourgeat did so. Edith was not yet up, and she was usually a tiger when wakened. But she didn't scare Jacques. From

In her room at Pigalle.

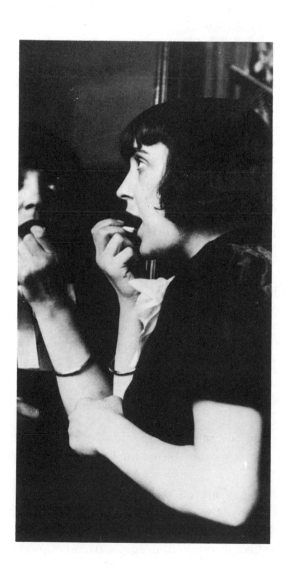

The Abbey of Port-Royal in the valley of the Chevreuse, where Edith and the poet-composer Jacques Bourgeat used to spend weekends.

then on, he often came by Gernys after three in the morning to pick her up, and they would go off and for a few francs share a dinner of soup and steak in Pigalle, usually at the Sans-Souci.

Edith began to earn a decent living at Gernys. With money in hand, she discovered a new passion: hats. She loved hats. The first one she bought cost ten francs—two or three dollars—at the Uniprix (the French equivalent of Woolworth's). It had five multicolored pompons. Jacques Bourgeat confessed: "When she strolled down the Avenue Clichy with that thing on her head, and either a sailor or soldier on her arm, I would ask her to walk either fifty feet in front of me or fifty feet behind. No way was I going to be found walking with such a couple!"

Bourgeat often went with Edith to a little hotel in the Chevreuse Valley, not far from the Abbey of Port-Royal-des-Champs. He used to read to her. Once while reading to her about the death of Socrates, of whose existence she had till that moment been totally unaware, she burst into tears.

"One day as we were walking she asked me the name of a flower she saw: they were morning glories. I told her they blossomed in the morning and closed at night. After dinner, she asked if we could go and check to see if the morning glories had in fact closed. We did, and for a long moment she stood gazing at the closed flowers. She said nothing, but half an hour later, back in her room, I could hear her sobbing her heart out."

Edith, like the flowers, blossomed through Bourgeat's friendship. As

44

long as she lived, she wrote him letters, opening her heart to him. After her death, he bequeathed the letters to the Bibliothèque Nationale, with the stipulation that they would only be made public in 2004. Here, though, is an extract from one that she wrote him from Lausanne, while she was touring in 1936:

Edith, being interrogated by the French police after Leplée's murder.

> I'm enclosing a photograph, for I'm still half asleep. So you can see that I don't look all that bad. I'm not with anyone anymore. I cut off all relations, for I've made up my mind to become serious and work very hard. . . . And when I come back to Paris I intend to remain alone. . . . I've decided I'm going to learn how to write properly, so that I don't make any more silly mistakes. You'll teach me, and you'll see what a good student I am. I want you to know that I'll also be going to the dentist, and that I plan to join a physical fitness course. You'll see how much your little bird has changed.

Louis Leplée's murder was an absurd crime, a bad joke turned tragic.
One Sunday morning in April 1936, Leplée sold an apartment he owned just off the Champs-Elysées. Without thinking, he bragged about the terrific sale he had made—"for 20,000 francs cash, my friends"—to some people at Gernys. Since it was Saturday and the banks were closed, it was obvious the money was still in his possession.
Four young hoods who were hanging around Gernys that day paid

45

Leplée an unexpected visit about four o'clock Sunday morning, intent on relieving him of his 20,000 francs. They passed a maid on the stairway going up, and tweaked her gallantly on the cheek, which seems to indicate that murder was far from their minds. Leplée doubtless panicked. In any case, a revolver was fired in the scuffle, and Louis was shot in the head. He died instantly. For nothing.

Although he had been Edith's benefactor and protector, she was among the suspects. Like Leplée, she was known to hang around with hoods and unsavory characters.

One should remember that Piaf's meteoric rise to fame during the six-month period following her debut at Gernys came at a time when there were no long-playing records, and no television, and that her fame was totally dependent on the *Tout Paris*—an in-crowd that was cruel, superficial and fickle—which was still not quite comfortable with, and terrified by, this poor kid who smelled of the streets and whose voice rose straight from the gutter.

In those days Piaf's public, like that of Charlie Chaplin, but obviously on a much smaller scale, was affected by her own background and that of the children of her class. When Piaf sang of poverty and misery and an unhappy childhood she made her listeners cry. But their tears dried quickly.

Kid Piaf, flanked by two French policemen, in front of the door to Leplée's apartment.

Several journalists got as much mileage as they could out of the Leplée affair by trying to implicate Edith in it. One of the few who defended her was Marcel Montarron. Writing in the magazine *Détective* on April 16, 1936, Montarron noted:

The man in the street has no idea who Louis Leplée is. But he does know Edith Piaf, whose name and voice have often been heard on the radio. Today Kid Piaf is surrounded and assailed by newspaper reporters. Not because of her singing but because of her connection to Louis Leplée, who was recently murdered. Leplée discovered Piaf, and helped launch her career. When she learned of his death, she fainted. The Kid is little more than skin and bones, and at the least provocation breaks down and sobs. Yet they won't let her alone: they barrage her with questions. Does she have any idea who might have done it? No, she doesn't have the faintest notion, but then she drops the name of an ex-lover, Henri Vallette, and the next minute thinks out loud that maybe Georges of the Foreign Legion, whom she met not long ago and had a brief flirtation with, maybe it could have been Georges, or maybe it's the guy she's with right now. . . .

At Leplée's funeral. Edith in the front row, wearing the black stockings, near collapse.

The last-named was a young sailor named Pierrot. "You have no idea how stupid he is!" said Piaf one night when she was eating frogs' legs for the first time in her life, in the company of Montarron and photo-jour-

47

Piaf often sang in the courtyards of the apartment houses in the best sections of Paris.

nalist Jean-Gabriel Serruzier, who was responsible for the remarkable photographs of Piaf at the time of the Leplée affair, seen here.

Piaf never forgot that period of her life. Actually, she had an elephantine memory. She had the ability to turn people on at will, and it was a talent she employed as often as she liked. She couldn't bear happy couples. In fact, there were a great many things she couldn't bear. Her early life had been too tough, and the world she sang about too unjust. As Montarron wrote later in *Voilà*:

> Kid Piaf was capable of singing the most patriotic songs, such as *Sambre-et-Meuse*, to a bunch of soldiers at a concert in the barracks in the afternoon, and that same evening the *Internationale* to a bunch of miners in a workers' café. And these black-faced miners would sit mesmerized by this skinny, pale-faced kid from Paris who, from her table-top perch where they had hoisted her, sang to them of revolt and better days to come.

For Edith there was no contradiction, and if in those days she sang of revolution, she didn't do it for very long. She very soon realized that what she could do best, and what she cared about most, were the songs that dealt with broken hearts.

As soon as she had enough to eat, her whole focus shifted to love. And what she loved best about love was its pain and suffering; she loved what could make her transcend herself. She never found anything better than love—unhappy love—to sing about. In 1950 she wrote and sang a song:

At the time of Leplée's murder, many of Edith's so-called friends abandoned her. Among those who did not were Juel, her accordionist; Raymond Asso the composer; and Marcel Montarron, the only journalist who stood up for her throughout the affair.

I loved a man so much, so much.
He loved me scarcely.
Life's not worth much, not much.
I killed him. Tough for me.[5]

Commissioner Guillaume, who was heading the investigation into Leplée's murder, knew very well that Edith was not involved, but he

50

wanted to take advantage of her emotional vulnerability to see what information he might glean about the activities of the petty hoods she hung around with in Pigalle and Ménilmontant.

Edith broke down and began to sob. First, because she was genuinely broken-hearted by Leplée's death, and second because once again she found herself confronted by life's injustice. She who had dreamed so often of seeing her name in headlines now found her dream realized, but her name was being dragged through the mud.

CAFE SINGER IMPLICATED IN THE LEPLEE AFFAIR.
CABARET STAR'S REAL NAME ISN'T PIAF.
WHERE THERE'S SMOKE THERE'S FIRE.

Leplée too was suffering a final injustice. His many "friends" were afraid to be seen at his funeral. Only a few faithful showed up. Edith, barely able to control her sobbing, clung to the arm of Laure Jarnys, who had once reigned at the cabaret Six Jours and was now a hostess/B-girl at Gernys.

"Your benefactor is dead," people cried out to her along the funeral route, "it's back to the streets for you, Kid!"

And all those who a few days before had feted and toasted her, dropped her brutally. All she had left was her superb voice, which she had not yet learned to control.

At this point in her life, Piaf almost slipped back into the gutter.

There were, nonetheless, a few who remained faithful: her accordionist, Juel, who was rewarded for his fidelity by being referred to as Edith's pimp; Jacques Bourgeat, who never failed her; Marguerite Monnot, the romantic, moody composer and musician who turned out to be one of the "angels" in Piaf's life; Jacques Canetti, who in those days worked for the French radio and was doing his best to get Edith singing spots on radio; and Raymond Asso, who would soon play a major role in Piaf's life.

Leplée's murder was only one of many curses which beset Edith's life. Curse or fate, many were those who whispered that she was responsible for it. People like Edith Piaf become objects of adoration bordering on idolatry, as well as incredible hatred. All stars know this; in Edith's case, she was throughout her life an idol accursed.

PIAF BRINGS BAD LUCK, screamed a headline in *France-Dimanche*. She was blamed for Cerdan's loss of a bout; it was her "evil eye" that made Cerdan's plane crash, as it had that of her young American lover, Douglas Davies. And in this instance, Leplée had been murdered because he had had the misfortune to allow her into Gernys.

4

ASSO

It was the others who killed her. She was so malleable, so easily influenced.

—Raymond Asso

I was with her for three years, and I could make her do whatever I wanted.

—Raymond Asso

My poor little girl . . . on the human level, a savage. She didn't know how to eat, she didn't know how to wash. . . .   —Raymond Asso

She resembled a Spanish beggar, one of those street kids who are as proud as they are disdainful, as timid as they are fearful.

—Raymond Asso

After Leplée's death, Canetti booked Edith on a tour of the neighborhood cinemas in Paris, which often had live entertainers as well. The tour didn't pan out very well. The workers resented the fact that one of their own, a lower-class girl, had gotten mixed up in a bourgeois crime that had overtones of a sex scandal. At the Odett Theater in Pigalle she was booed and insulted. She hated Paris. And she was afraid.

At that point Canetti talked about her to a young and upcoming impresario, Fernand Lumbroso. "Out in the provinces," he said, "the Leplée affair is less well known. Why don't you try and get some bookings for her there?"

Piaf arrived at Lumbroso's wearing her rabbit-fur coat, with a flat hat planted askew on her head, her hair in bangs. At her side was Momone, who had turned up again. Lumbroso, not quite sure of doing the right thing, booked them into a cinema in the port city of Brest. The girls found the town lugubrious, and began living it up with the local sailors. Edith often arrived late for her act, none too steady on her legs. Her repertoire included *Correcq et réguyer, le Grand Totor, la Fille et le Chien, Entre Saint-Ouen et Clignancourt,* and was introduced by Momone:

> Ladies and gentlemen, directly from Paris we bring you Kid Piaf, who will sing for you songs ranging from your old favorites to the latest love songs . . .

Piaf living it up with some friends in the big convertible.

Fernand Lumbroso, a young impresario on the way up. Because of the Leplée taint, France was cool to booking Piaf, so Lumbroso decided she might do better in Belgium. So off she went, with Momone in her wake.

The sailors were unimpressed, and the noise they made shucking peanuts almost drowned out Piaf. By the time she was finished the place looked more like a zoo than a theater. The middle-class patrons were upset, the manager furious. He lodged a complaint with Lumbroso, who took a deep breath and sent the girls on to Belgium, where their conduct was, if anything, worse. Thence to Nice, where he booked Edith into a nightclub called La Boîte à Vitesse. She wasn't earning much, was hanging around with a bunch of local hoods, and at one point went so far as to lock some American sailors in her room to make sure they'd still be there when she got back from work. She felt the whole world slowly sinking beneath her.

Nothing gave her pleasure anymore. Leplée's death struck her as a premonition of worse things to come. It was with a heavy heart, and fully as unhappy as the heroines of her songs, that she went back to Paris. And there, for some inexplicable reason, she experienced one of those extraordinary renewals of energy and purpose, brought about by and fo-

cused on her career, that were to occur many times during her life. She called on Raymond Asso for help. They had met briefly in October 1935, just as she was beginning her stint at Leplée's, in the corridors of a music publishing house where she had gone to find some songs to broaden her repertoire. Asso had just written his first song. When he met Piaf it was love at first sight. As he tells it, his life up to that point had been totally meaningless:

> I was a kid from North Africa, Morocco to be precise, and at fifteen I was still a shepherd there. At nineteen, a soldier. When I got out of the army in 1923, I held dozens of different jobs, all more or less crazy, before I straightened out. Morocco can do that to you: it's a very peculiar climate, a very peculiar world, that leaves its mark. But the day I met Piaf, all that early part of my life seemed meaningless.

Asso was petrified: he sensed that he had met his destiny. He would be but the first of many links in the Piaf chain, but actually the night they met it was she who scoured the cafés and clubs of Pigalle, asking if anyone had seen "a skinny guy with a big nose who lives around here and who writes songs."

If Piaf often made mistakes when it came to love, she had an absolutely sure instinct when she was looking for those needed to help advance her career, and it was with that same sure instinct—and that same cruelty—that she got rid of them when she felt the time had come to renew herself and her art.

A young man said he thought he knew the guy she was looking for and led her to Asso's room. He was writing a song that would soon take Paris by storm: *Mon Légionnaire.*

> *His eyes were big and bright*
> *With brilliant flashes in the blue*
> *Like storms on a summer night.*
> *He was covered with tattoos*
> *That I never fully understood.*
> *On his neck: "Not seen, not won"*
> *On his heart one read "No one"*
> *On his right arm, a word: "Reason."* [6]

Edith read the song. "It's not bad," she said, obviously not knocked out by it, "but I'd like it more if you made him a colonial soldier." She had no idea as she said that with what a heart-rending voice she would later sing:

> *Don't know his name,*
> *Know nothing about the guy,*
> *Loved me all night long*
> *My Legionnaire . . . .* [7]

It just so happened that her latest boyfriend was a colonial soldier.

Asso smiled. As yet, he was not offended by her remarks. The next day Edith took Marguerite Monnot to see him. It was she who would write the music for *Mon Légionnaire.*

Asso had already been bitten by the Piaf bug, but didn't want her to know it. Anyway, since she didn't want to sing his new song, he'd give it to Marie Dubas, another singer he knew who was on the rise.

Edith would later regret that she hadn't launched that song, but for the moment she was too caught up in her life at the rue Pierre-Charron and her nightly flings in Pigalle to worry. She kept away from Asso, who judged the people she was running around with very harshly. "Their idea of taking care of her," he remarked, "is to fill her full of Beaujolais and brandy."

She left for Nice, and for a while painted that town red. Then she headed north. From the train station she called Asso: "Raymond . . . I'm

(Opposite) Edith and Raymond Asso, who had just written the song that was soon to become famous, *Mon Légionnaire.* Edith turned it down because, just then, she was in love with a colonial soldier. "I used to call her Didou," Asso relates, "and she called me—God knows why!—Cyrano!"

58

Edith toured the south of France, and sang at the Bôite à Vitesse in Nice, where her high-jinks once again got her into trouble.

Meanwhile, in Paris, Joséphine Baker was taking the city by storm.

at the Gare de Lyon. I've just put my last coins into this pay phone. I don't have any more contracts. I've been thrown out of everywhere. I've been having a ball, Raymond, but now I don't know where to go or what to do. Tell me, Raymond. You're the only one who can save me. Either that or back to the street. What shall I do?" she said, her voice quivering, according to Asso. He didn't hesitate for a second. "Hop in a taxi, I'll be waiting for you," he said, his heart beating with joy.

He was to become her pimp, but he loved her.

She would end up demanding that he write solely for her. The Marie Dubas story had been a lesson to her. One of Edith's greatest strengths was to understand almost instinctively that her musicians and lyricists should write only for her. She went so far as to take them with her to America or anywhere else she traveled. She was all too aware of the dangers of absence. For her . . . but also for them.

Asso-the-Redeemer realized the extraordinary stroke of luck that Edith's phone call meant for him. He would manage to keep her only by beating her, and Momone—whom he would refer to thirty years later as "Edith's daily demon" —he sent packing. But he wrote for her, he fought for her, he forced her to buckle down and work.

"After having been through Asso's hands," said Paul Meurisse, the next lover, "Edith had become a highly trained horse."

Asso saw himself as the one destined to transform Edith from a caterpillar into a butterfly. He, who was crazy about the Kid, the little girl from the streets, would give birth to the star Piaf.

61

"I used to call her Didou," Asso noted. "For though it's true that I was reborn with her, I also know that I was the one who brought her into the world. People love to give childish nicknames to those they love. She often used to call me Cyrano."

Asso was obsessed by the idea that Edith had to become a star, had to have a triumph that would consecrate her once and for all. Mitty Goldin, the director of the A.B.C. Theater in Paris, wanted nothing to do with her. He'd heard all about her escapades and unreliability and for the time being, at least, he had all the singing stars he needed. This was the era of such great singers as Tino Rossi, Lucienne Boyer, Charles Trénet, Joséphine Baker, and Jean Lumière. The last thing Mitty Goldin needed, thank you very much, was this young girl fresh from the streets, this hellion who seemed to divide her time between soldiers and pimps.

But after a three months' struggle, after having made Edith work day and night, Asso emerged victorious. Edith Piaf was booked into the A.B.C. Theater for the spring of 1937, a one-woman show where she appeared dressed in a simple black dress with a white lace collar, her hair washed and combed, her face almost mystical.

The result was more than Asso had hoped for: a triumph. Not only a music-hall triumph, but a musical triumph as well. Edith Piaf was on her way.

Asso, flushed with victory, asked Lumbroso to break his contract with Edith. Anyway, he pointed out slyly, the contract wasn't legally binding. Piaf was still a minor! "Besides, I'm the one who wakes her up in the morning and brings her her morning tea, I'm the one who takes care of her, who cleans her up when she . . . if she . . . I'm the one who washes her when she throws up."

He said all those things to conceal the one real truth, that he was madly in love with her. Piaf knew that she needed him, that his consuming passion was essential for her career, that his authority and leadership were working constantly on her behalf.

She realized it but that didn't mean she submitted docilely to the situation. Many were the nights that Raymond had to roam the streets of Pigalle looking for her. Edith was fully aware of the destructive, evil forces within her.

"Stick with me," she would tell him, "don't let me go, and I promise that I'll do everything you ask me to. I don't want to go back to the gutter, but I'll never be able to make it all by myself. There's too much in me that's bad, but I never hear it when you're with me."

She swore on everything that was holy how obedient she would be . . . and then she'd run away.

But she also worked . . . and she got better. Her artistic instincts were

In the spring of 1937, Edith appeared in a one-woman show at the A.B.C. Theater, and scored a major triumph. Her black dress, with the little lace collar, was her trademark.

Also in 1937, the lst of May brought a big turnout of discontented workers, demanding their rights.

sure, and she also had a will of iron when needed. She had a great voice, true, but what she had in addition was a knowledge gleaned from her years in the streets. "Piaf was a complete artist," noted Pierre Hiégel, who had known her when she was only thirteen. "A total, absolute artist, but at that time she didn't yet know it. Professionally, she is certainly the most astonishing talent the music-hall world has ever produced."

She was so strong it was not long before the pupil excelled her teacher. But without doubt those two years of tough training and discipline are the key to her talent and the stringent discipline that marked her professional life. Asso put her back on her feet, but their years together were stormy. In 1938, Edith wrote him from Chenevelles:

My dear love,

How much it must have cost you to write me such awful things. But you're right, I am stupid. I always told you I was, and you tried to convince me that I was intelligent. Besides, the fact that I did all those dumb things before I met you only proves my lack of intelligence, and

it's high time I made amends to all the people I hurt through the years. The very thought makes me want to cry bitter tears of shame and regret. . . . But you're going too far to say all the things you said in your letter. I hate myself, and I have no confidence in myself whatsoever.

Of course, Asso's insults were a kind of love letter to Edith. But she, who spent her life singing of unhappy and unrequited love, found it very difficult to put up with the kind of exclusivity Asso's passion demanded.

As twenty years earlier war had taken Edith's father away, so now another war took Asso too. He was called up on August 4, 1939. Only days before a concert that Edith was scheduled to give in Deauville, that Asso had arranged for her, he was inducted and sent to join an army regiment in Digne.

Edith had just sung at the Bobino Theater in Paris, and that too had been a triumph. The entire program had been of songs by Raymond Asso, without doubt the longest love letter he ever wrote.

War clouds were gathering. In August 1939, Asso was called up into military service.

65

"I knew that I was helping shape something great, something monumental," he lamented thirty years after he had lost her.

By the time he was demobilized a few months later, Edith had already slipped back into her undisciplined ways. She had reinstated Momone in her life; in fact, Momone was living in Asso's room in the Hotel Alsina where Edith was living. There was also a newcomer in Edith's room, Paul Meurisse. A singer and nightclub artist, Meurisse had graduated from the chorus—he was the letter G, surrounded by eight Blue Bell Girls, in an act entitled "Revue du Rire" at the A.B.C. Theater—in a show starring Marie Dubas. Now he was singing at the Amiral, a nightclub not far from the one where Edith was performing.

Edith had never lost her obsession for independence, and now she reverted to the girl she had been at fifteen. She now was famous, she had a profession, so it was time to laugh and have a good time. For though she made her career singing of misery and unhappiness, there was in Piaf an element of deep-seated gaiety, a desire to have fun and goof off and play dumb tricks if they were good for laughs. Since life had refused her a childhood, she would fabricate one for herself and do all the silly things she had never had a chance to do when she was little.

There were times when it could have cost her dearly. During the German Occupation, for instance, she and Momone would go out drinking, and by six in the afternoon they would be dead drunk, playing leap-frog on the Avenue Carnot. Or she and her "dark angel" would seek out the longest street in Paris they could find and stop off in every café from one end to the other, offering drinks on the house to everyone inside at each stop. They would end up the evening crawling along the rue de Belleville on all fours. Twenty years later, Piaf would sing:

> *If one day you up and left me,*
> *Just departed,*
> *Leaving me alone, bereft,*
> *I can tell you that I'd die,*
> *Die alone and broken hearted.*[8]

After Louis Leplée, and after her own father—the human-pretzel man, the man who could walk on his hands—she next eliminated her third father, Raymond Asso.

The little street-girl, the little girl with forget-me-not eyes of blue, was implacable.

"Madame Piaf is a star
who is burning herself out
in the nocturnal sky of
France." *Jean Cocteau.*

5

COCTEAU

A magnificent gigolo, on the
verge of no longer being so.
  —Jean Cocteau, describing
    the character of *Le Bel
    Indifférent*

Perhaps she and Cocteau did
talk to each other about
death near the end of their
lives. They used to talk on
the telephone every day, but
I never listened to what they
were saying.
              —Théo Sarapo

Madame Piaf is a genius.
She is inimitable. There
never was anyone like her,
and there will never be
another Edith Piaf.
              —Jean Cocteau

Your face, that my hands
want to learn by heart.
              —Jean Cocteau

She found songs that aimed
at a high level but never lost
their popular origins, or
popular appeal.
              —Paul Meurisse

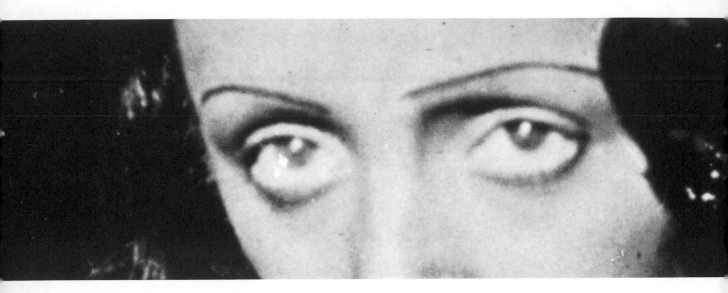

In the space of a few short months Edith had become the toast of Paris, especially the intellectuals. Jean Cocteau was captivated by her and often came to hear her sing. They soon became very close: there was a deep feeling between them. "Teach her to read?" Cocteau used to say. "No need to. She already knows what she reads." As fate would have it, she and Cocteau died the same day, and the world was quick to note the disparity between the two funerals: Edith's, with tens of thousands in attendance, and almost no one at Cocteau's. The poet wouldn't have taken umbrage at the public slight. He was too fond of Edith, too entranced by her talent.

> Look at that tiny person whose hands are those of a lizard. Look at her Bonaparte brow, at her eyes, like those of a blind person who has just regained her sight. How will she sing? How will she express herself? How will that tiny chest give birth to songs of sorrow that touch the heart? . . .
>
> And then she begins to sing, and you hear a voice that wells up from the depths of her being, a voice that dwells within her from head to toe, a voice that unfolds like a tall wave of black velvet.

Piaf was busy rehearsing Cocteau's play *Le Bel Indifférent* with Paul Meurisse as her costar. Shortly before the first night, Meurisse was called up into the army as well. Piaf, who was never afraid of anyone or anything, wrote to the Minister of War and requested that Meurisse's induction be delayed long enough for him to be present for the opening night. On the envelope she had scrawled: "To the Personal Attention of the Minister of War, from Madame Edith Piaf." Meurisse was granted a ten-day delay.

Piaf was prodigious in *Le Bel Indifférent*. Paul Meurisse is unfair. "Piaf

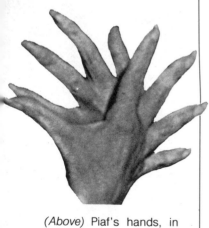

was a very poor comedienne. De Gaulle wasn't a singer, but he sang the *Marseillaise* very well indeed. *Le Bel Indifférent* was Piaf's *Marseillaise.*"

He was less prejudiced when he talked about her as a singer: "Her voice was a cry of love. Her hands: when they lay there next to her body, white against the black dress, they were perfection. Her faith: she radiated it, as though she had just stepped out of a painting by El Greco."

Paul Meurisse, a bank director's son, was born into an upper middle-class family of Flemish origins who had settled in Aix-en-Provence. As a young man he had worked as a notary's clerk, but the day he saw Rudolph Valentino in *The Black Eagle* he knew that he could never accept any other life but that of show business.

He spent several middling years as a singer before becoming a great actor. He first caught Edith's eye in the nightclub where she was performing. He was a good-looking man, a cross between Valentino and Buster Keaton. There was also an air about him of a high-class hood that appealed to and charmed Edith.

"At twenty-five," he said, "Edith had a pure face, a pert little nose; in short, she was very pretty."

With Meurisse, Edith experienced her first adventure with the finer things of life. He brought her down from Montmartre to the elegance of the Etoile. She left the Hotel Alsina where she had lived with Raymond Asso to live with Meurisse in an apartment—her first—at 10 bis, rue Anatole de la Forge. He tried to teach her proper manners, and they fought like cats and dogs. Several times she broke every piece of china in the house, and he kicked a radio to death. Every time Edith felt she might have met her master, she fought back like a tiger. She rebelled against any love-prison. It was enough that she sang about love.

The journalists went overboard for Edith in writing about her performance in *Le Bel Indifférent*. The fact is, she was always grist for the critics' mill, and she continually fascinated them. The theater reviewer for *Comoedia* wrote:

> She acts the way one dies, perhaps without knowing how well she does it. . . . Piaf's great talent is love. . . . With her wild hair, looking for all the world like a harridan, her tiny body clothed in demonic black, Piaf is a priestess of love.

Priestess of love! Maybe everywhere else but certainly not in her personal life. Her love affair with Paul Meurisse gave birth to a number of anecdotes that form an essential part of the folklore of "Piaf and Men." Piaf said: "As far as I'm concerned, love means fighting, big fat lies, and a couple of slaps across the face."

Meurisse had had his fill. One night, during the German Occupation, after Tino Rossi had acted as mediator and reconciled the two battling

lovers, they were on their way home in a horse-drawn cab—there were practically no cars left in Paris in those days. Edith found some pretext to start another fight, and before long they were at it again tooth and nail in the cab. When they arrived home, Meurisse literally lifted Edith out of the cab, laid her on the sidewalk, holding her down with one foot, while he paid the cabbie.

During the night, she said to him: "You have some pretty strange ways of mounting me, you know!"

Two years before, in 1937, Piaf had already played a supporting role in a Jean de Limur film starring Marie Bell, entitled *La Garçonne.* While she was still with Meurisse, Georges Lacombe offered her a lead role in a film called *Montmartre-sur-Seine,* whose costars included Jean-Louis Barrault, Serge Reggiani, Georges Marchal, and Paul Meurisse. Although she and Paul were on the verge of breaking up, that film—which was a lemon—prolonged their relationship by several weeks.

The scenario, written by André Cayatte, told the story of a girl who worked in a flower shop and who became a big star. The story was obviously loosely modeled on Piaf's own meteoric rise to fame. The film was a flop, but through it she met another poet, Jacques Audiberti, who was also the film critic for the film magazine *Comoedia.*

Audiberti had never met Piaf, yet he wrote of her that she was built like "one of those forks you eat oysters with," and said that when she opened her mouth she became "one of the most touching and heart-rending of artists, who in the space of a few brief minutes can give us a glimpse of the heights, as well as the depths, of life." He went on:

> The demon of the cinema politely gives way to allow that very special phenomenon who does not fit into the family to make its way. Such a person is Edith Piaf, who has the ability and the power to peel away the extraneous and move straight to the public's heart.

In *Je suis partout* the critic Lucien Rebattet wrote "although her triviality has the merit of not being ghetto-phony, there is no explaining why they felt compelled to make this physically unimposing person, with her oversized, macabre head hunched in her round shoulders and her cavernous eyes, even more sickly than she really is."

All this in the depths of the German Occupation, and the gray streets of occupied Paris are filled with the images of the Nazi presence.

Paris under the Germans. Edith still performs, and triumphs, at the A.B.C. Theater.

Madame Billy, who ran
the brothel/hotel on the
rue de Villejust where
Edith lived during the war.

6
WARS AND BROTHELS

Every time she raised so
much hell, or made so much
noise that the neighbors
would complain, I'd simply
tell them: "It's Madame Piaf
rehearsing." "Oh, in that
case it's all right."   —Billy

She never really knew
precisely what it was she
wanted.   —Billy

When she sang, it was a
whole other Edith.   —Billy

It was at this time that a woman named Andrée Bigard came into Piaf's life. She acted as her secretary from 1940 to 1950, and was always a positive influence. "It was Bigard who taught her proper manners," said Billy, who as recently as a few months ago still ran her "house" on the rue Paul-Valéry.

In the course of her life, Piaf experienced two wars and two brothels. Of the brothels, the first was her grandmother's in Bernay, where she lived happily until she was seven. Nineteen years later, she rang Billy's doorbell, who then had a brothel on the rue de Villejust. Edith and Andrée Bigard lived there until the Liberation.

Today Billy is still a superb woman, with piercing blue porcelain eyes that gleam with malice. She showed me the police registers: Edith lived with her from 1942 to 1944.

"Do you remember the first time you saw Piaf?"

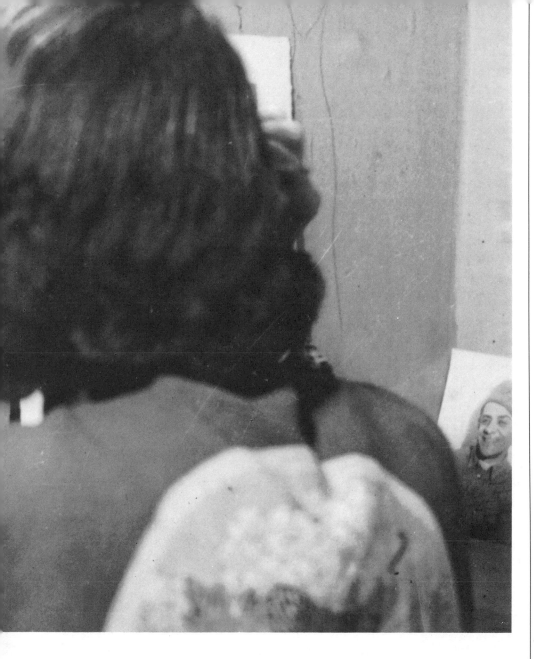

"Do I ever! She stole six pairs of shoes from me!"

Actually, it was Momone who took the six pairs of expensive alligator shoes that belonged to Madame Sée, Billy's associate, who was later deported by the Germans and never returned. She took the shoes up to Montmartre and sold them on the black market for a handsome price.

The rue de Villejust wasn't far from the rue Lauriston, where the Gestapo headquarters in Paris were located. But though Billy trafficked in the black market, and though a lot of Germans visited her establishment, she concealed Jews and the possessions of Jewish friends.

Edith was already a big star.

Billy rented her the entire third floor, where she lived with Bigard and Momone, who frequently absconded with the contents of Edith's closet to sell on the black market.

On the same floor lived a washed-up singer who was madly in love with Piaf. He used to go to sleep at night, a cross on his chest, praying, "Please, God, make me a male Piaf!"

Sometimes Edith would descend the stairs on her hands, her dress tumbling down over her head. "No question that she picked that up as a kid when she performed with her father!"

And the endless escapades with Momone continued. "She was her real pimp," said Madame Billy.

One day during the Occupation someone knocked at the door and reported that there were two nude young ladies standing at the window on the third floor, and that the passers-by were staring at them. Billy bounded up the stairs four at a time and discovered Piaf and Momone at the window, their arms crossed in front of them.

"Mademoiselle Edith, be reasonable!" she implored. "People can see you from the street."

"Billy, don't be angry. I've done something bad and I'm punishing myself. I have to stand this way for five hours."

In the end, Billy won a concession. Edith and Momone remained standing exactly as she had found them, for the allotted number of hours, but now behind the closed shutters.

When Piaf met Billy, she was in the habit of chewing garlic and playing dice. Andrée Bigard recalls to this day the smell of garlic that permeated the room whenever she went in to open the shutters.

Bigard, a slight, intelligent woman bursting with energy, bought Edith her first brassiere, in 1940. For Edith it was a prison, an unbearable choker, and whenever she would bow at the end of a performance she would reach behind with her hands and unfasten it, like a naughty schoolgirl.

"One day," Bigard smiled, "she forgot it."

During Piaf's stay at the rue de Villejust—today renamed rue Paul-Valéry—there was a piano in the living room and another on the third floor, in Piaf's room. In the early days of her comeback, Edith was able to live and blossom in the kind of marginal situation she needed so badly. Besides, she had discovered the gimmick she needed to exorcise all her problems, a gift that Asso had left her when he left for the army: work. If she didn't work like a slave, she castigated herself unmercifully. It was what she needed. She was as much a masochist as she was a perfectionist. Billy showed me the glass door through which

Where did her fascination with pimps come from? Was it from her years at her grandmother's in Bernay, or her nocturnal street life in Pigalle years later?

80

Asso had thrown Edith at one point. "That was the only language she understood: physical violence. She had an innate need to be dominated, tamed," she went on. She recalled one dinner where, among others, the guests included Michel Simon, Jean Cocteau, and Henri Contet, whom Piaf had met during the shooting of *Montmartre-sur-Seine*. Contet was a critic for the film revue *Cinémondial* and had been the publicity director for that film. At that time he was Piaf's "favorite." The atmosphere during dinner was very tense and unpleasant. Piaf was impossible. At one point Billy whispered to Contet: "Why don't you take her up and indulge her vice a bit, just so she won't ruin our evening." Ten minutes later they were back down. "He had given her a couple of good hard slaps," Billy smiled. "Both her cheeks were bright pink. After that she was sweet and charming and happy."

Billy's husband, whose name was Josselin, was also a singer, and he often toured with Piaf. Just before she left for a three-month tour in the south, Edith took Billy aside.

"I have to talk to you, Billy."

"I'm listening, Mademoiselle Edith."

"All right, here it is. We're leaving for three months. This time I want your husband to be completely at my service. Do you understand what I mean? Not only during the day but at night too. I'm going to take your place. I'll make a star out of him. You have forty-eight hours to give me your answer."

"I've already thought about it," Billy replied stoically. "The answer is no, Mademoiselle Edith."

Thirty-five years after the event she sighed and said: "Maybe I was wrong. She *did* launch the careers of so many men!"

At Billy's, Piaf was like a fish in water. She could clown around at ten in the evening singing classical music and then, at two or three in the morning, call for her pianist or accordionist "to work." That nocturnal tyranny was apparently ingrained: she needed an antidote to chase away the terrors of the night.

During the war, bicycle taxicabs were the order of the day. When Edith left the rue de Villejust on tour, accompanied by Billy's husband, they took a bicycle-cab to the station.

81

Piaf had plenty of ghosts to exorcise. Was it at Bernay or later in Pigalle that she discovered her attraction to pimps, which would follow her to the end, wherever she went? It's true that at twenty, given the background and upbringing that had been hers, acceptance in the underworld was a promotion, a big step above the utter poverty of her childhood. Piaf would always be fascinated—or would pretend to be fascinated—by hoods and petty gangsters, and to be touched by whores. "I gave her my fur coat. Making her living that way she needs it more than I do."

Tenderness. Identification. With Edith, nothing was simple. She played the whore. She forced people to let her down and abandon her. Yet the truth was that she abandoned them. She was always the other face of the victim, and she sang about it:

> She hung around the rue Pigalle
> She smelled of inexpensive vice
> And reeked of sin. She wasn't nice
> This pale and scrawny two-bit gal.[9]

Fate only struck Edith in her early years. Later, she became her own destiny. And, as she lay dying, when she said to her nurse, "I'm paying dearly for my stupidities, aren't I?" she was absolutely right.

Piaf in her dressing room, with a picture of Maurice Chevalier on her dressing table.

In Sacha Guitry's wartime film, *Si Versailles m'était conté,* Edith sang *La Carmagnole.*

7

THE OCCUPATION

The song *Le Fanion de la Légion* is part and parcel of my basic repertoire. If you don't want me to sing it, you'll have to ban it.
— Edith Piaf

At the time of the Liberation, she said: "You know what I'd like to see? I'd like to see one person—just one—who would own up to having been a coward."

Edith, as the godmother of Stalag III D, made several trips to the prisoner-of-war camp, to entertain the troops. Here she is being helped from an army truck upon her arrival.

However strange it may seem, the war years were a positive and productive period for Piaf. Never had she been in better shape physically; never had she been funnier or in a better frame of mind; and never had she been surer of her own abilities.

Thanks to Henri Contet, she had plenty of work. She changed her style; she progressed. Her way of taking part in the Resistance was to have a Jewish lover, the Polish pianist Norbert Glanzberg, who was a fine musician himself and whose legacy to her was a deeper knowledge and appreciation of music. He also knew how to keep Edith happy: he beat her to a pulp, as prescribed. Edith also befriended and helped another Jewish musician, Michel Emer, who wrote for her one of her most famous songs, *The Accordionist*, before he was drafted and sent off to serve during the "phony war," when the French still firmly believed the Maginot Line was their sure line of defense.

86

Piaf was completely apolitical, and her reaction to the Occupation was that of a Parisian street kid.

> *Hitler? Can't stand his guts,*
> *Can't bear that man.*
> *The Nazis seem to have forgot*
> *That when we fought them last,*
> *We wiped them out!* [10]

That was a song she was singing three years before World War II broke out.

Most French actors and singers—unless they were Jewish—kept on working under the German Occupation, and only a very few, who had clearly collaborated too closely with the Nazis, were brought to judgment at the Liberation.

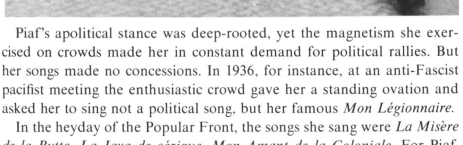

Walking in Berlin with her colleagues Fred Adison, Charles Trenet, her pianist, and her secretary-companion, Andrée Bigard.

Piaf's apolitical stance was deep-rooted, yet the magnetism she exercised on crowds made her in constant demand for political rallies. But her songs made no concessions. In 1936, for instance, at an anti-Fascist pacifist meeting the enthusiastic crowd gave her a standing ovation and asked her to sing not a political song, but her famous *Mon Légionnaire*.

In the heyday of the Popular Front, the songs she sang were *La Misère de la Butte, La Java de cézigue, Mon Amant de la Coloniale*. For Piaf, unhappiness was the misfortune of birth, the despair of unrequited love, of sailors who don't return and soldiers of the Foreign Legion who die for flag and country. She wallowed in fatalism and misery, and steadfastly resisted all efforts to get her involved in any political movement or party.

She had always resisted any political song, and the closest she ever came was in Sacha Guitry's film recreating the French Revolution, where she sang the patriotic *La Carmagnole*. She loved to sing about the army, about soldiers and sailors and tough old veterans. She evolved from a childhood where being hungry was par for the course to the woman in love whose man has jilted her, but she never held society responsible for either problem.

René Rouzaud, a songwriter whose Piaf hits included *La Goualante du pauvre Jean* and who also wrote the lyrics for many of Yves Montand's songs, used to say about Piaf:

> She sang of a world long gone. She sang of the heroes and heroines in the popular serialized novels, of the stereotypes that filled them, and in every instance she breathed new life into them. The solutions she pro-

A prisoner-of-war drawing Piaf's portrait.

During a visit to Stalag III, Edith ran into an old pal from Belleville.

posed were escape, intense love, and fatalism. She belonged to the world of tramps and beggars. The proletariat was totally foreign to her. She respected it, while being afraid of it. Without question, she conferred an extraordinary grandeur on all her characters, whether a soldier of the Foreign Legion, a sailor, or a lady of the night. But today the soldier demands, and gets, a well-paid contract to do the Legion's dirty work; the sailor's a dues-paying member of a union, and the whore that Francis Carco wrote about years ago, who asked for a pittance for her services, today asks for ten thousand francs for a "short-time" job. The legends are dead and gone!

In 1940, Piaf became the godmother of a stalag: Stalag III. Thanks to her secretary, Andrée Bigard, who unlike Edith was a true member of the French Resistance, she managed to accomplish a number of heroic acts during the war, all done with that complete lack of awareness that was so typical of her. The most notable was the way in which they helped some French prisoners escape from the German camp, as members of Edith's orchestra. Andrée organized each phase of the operation in minute detail.

90

During Edith's first visit to Stalag III to entertain the prisoners—code-named Operation Seduction—they brought with them all sorts of presents for both the male and female guards: canned goods, Cognac, silk stockings.

Edith sang, and was a tremendous success. Even the Germans were ecstatic. The prisoners asked their guards for permission to be photographed with their "godmother." Meanwhile, Andrée was busy chatting with the prisoners, asking them for their addresses, "so that we could send word to their families that they were well." Then, once back in Paris, Andrée used those pictures taken at the Stalag to make up false identity cards, complete with address and photograph.

In the course of the second trip to the prisoner-of-war camp, they brought back the counterfeit I.D. cards, concealed in canned goods. The escaped prisoners would sneak aboard the train just before it reached the border. When the German police came through to check papers, Edith told them the men were part of her orchestra. Andrée Bigard got her own husband out of the Stalag in this way.

Here again, Edith, as in everything she undertook, was in search of her childhood, rather, the childhood she never had. Sneaking prisoners out of German camps was, for her, like playing hide-and-seek.

Momone was in and out of Piaf's life. She too was in search of her childhood, but her quest was compounded by the fact that she wasn't Edith Piaf, and therefore it often took diabolical—and sometimes dangerous—turns. In this classic love-hate relationship, Momone was obsessed with bringing her "sister" down in one way or another.

She not only entertained at prisoner-of-war camps, but also at labor camps, where Frenchmen who had been sent to work in Germany were housed. Here she performs in the final number of a show at a labor camp near Munich.

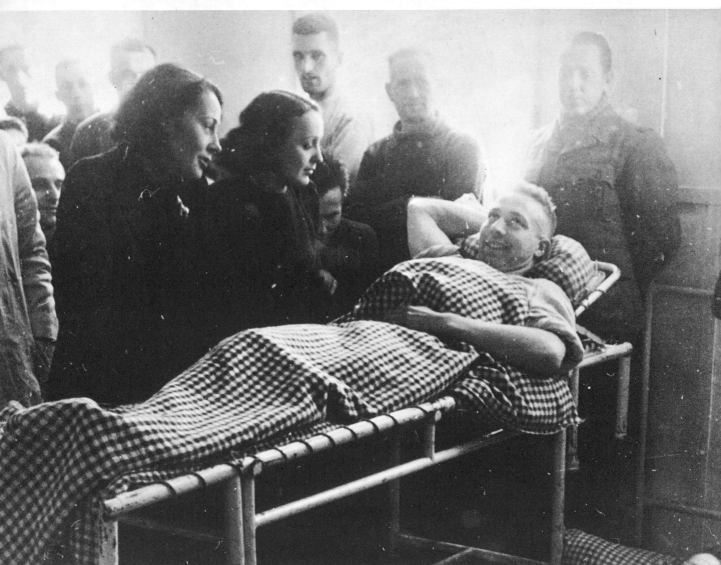

In one instance, when Momone knew that Edith was making a valiant effort to stay on the wagon and did not allow a drop of alcohol in the house, she not only hid a bottle of Cognac in the bathroom, but also made sure to let Edith know it was there. Piaf, in the words of Oscar Wilde, was able to resist anything except temptation, and all her enemies were well aware of it.

Besides, Momone, who had more than one trick up her sleeve, was a born comic. No one could make Edith laugh the way she could, and for that quality Piaf forgave her a great deal. She had, in fact, a great deal to forgive.

As a friend of Edith's, Momone had easy access to Billy's, and she often went there, even when Edith was away. Andrée Bigard more than once discovered that after these visits either money or clothing was missing. But Edith didn't want to hear about it; even if she was aware of it, she preferred to overlook it.

During the Occupation, all of Piaf's songs—as well as those of every other singer in France—had to be submitted to the censor's office. As a result, Bigard came to know a number of German officials. One afternoon, as she arrived back home from doing some shopping, she was greeted by Chang, their Chinese cook, who was beside himself:

"They just arrested Miss Edith!"

"Who did?"

"The Germans."

Bigard knew instinctively that Momone somehow was involved. She immediately telephoned her "friends" in the censor's office and soon located Edith. She hurried to the address they had given her and introduced herself as Mademoiselle Piaf's secretary. She found Edith in good spirits, her eyes sparkling with humor, in an office with two members of the Gestapo.

"Dédé," Edith began, "you always told me that I'd never be rich. Well, you were wrong! I've just learned that I own a yacht in Marseille, which I use to smuggle young Frenchmen into England!"

Without losing her cool for a second, Bigard furnished the Germans with a complete rundown of Edith's tours in the unoccupied zone of France, with full itineraries, and demonstrated she had never even been to Marseille. That was all the Germans wanted to know. Before they left, Edith invited both men to come and hear her sing at the Perroquet, where she was then appearing, and both were delighted to accept.

Bigard was certain that during one of her visits to Piaf's room, Momone had come across some incriminating papers, and had decided to use them to bring Edith down. When Bigard tried to explain her theory to Edith, to reconstruct the whole incident, Edith simply shook her head. She just didn't want to know about it.

(Opposite, above) Piaf photographed with prisoners after a performance. *(Opposite, below)* Chatting with a wounded soldier in a military hospital in Germany, 1944.

93

8

MONTAND

I called her one day. I had just finished writing a song for Maurice Chevalier: *Ma gosse, ma petite môme.* She burst into tears on the phone. "Don't give it to Chevalier," she implored. "Keep it for Yves."
—Henri Contet

She needed love: she sang well only when she was either euphoric or depressed. In love, she was the purest, simplest woman alive: before she got into bed she would always get down on her knees and pray. You can't picture Messalina saying her prayers in her nightgown.
—Yves Montand

Piaf and Yves Montand in Marcel Blistène's 1945 film, *Etoile sans lumière*.

(Opposite) In the newly liberated Paris, Yves and Edith are photographed before their charity performance at the 1945 *Bal des Petits Lits Blancs*.

Yves Montand was the son of Italian immigrants. Since the age of thirteen he had been working in Marseille, first in a spaghetti factory, then as a stevedore in the port.

Sundays he often sang at local parties or at workers' events, and when he didn't he would often visit his sister, who was a hairdresser. As the proud possessor of a permanent curler, she was not above trying out her electric marvel on Yves' lush locks.

Montand loved to sing cowboy songs written for him by a blind French composer, Charles Humel. His two idols were Fred Astaire and Charles Trenet. Locally, Montand had enough success to decide to go up to Paris and try his luck in the big city. He arrived there in 1944, and appeared at the A.B.C. Theater, where he was greeted as a "greaser" because of his loud checked jacket which, some time later, Piaf would get rid of—posthaste.

When Montand arrived in Paris, Piaf was already a big star, but the macho big-shot kid from Marseille was not about to kowtow to any female, even the Great Piaf. Still, one of his first jobs was in the chorus of the Moulin Rouge, "holding a spear," in a show starring none other than Piaf. If she wanted to discover him, she would have to do the looking.

96

Her reaction to meeting him was astonishing. With that absolutely sure instinct that she always possessed, she sensed immediately in him the Montand to come. Never one to mince words, she stripped him bare and analyzed him with an implacable lucidity. She told him that his American-style songs only worked in the present environment, while Paris was still occupied by the Germans. "As soon as they leave," she said, "the French won't give a damn about your Wild West and your hot-dog vendors in Central Park." Then she looked at his hands, which already set her to dreaming, and added: "Those hands of yours: they're worker's hands. They come from the people, and you have to make sure the people know it."

Montand bowed his head. He had found his master. Piaf made him work for hours on end with a pencil between his teeth, to make him lose his accent. She was going to let him in on every one of her secrets, for if Piaf was incredibly domineering when it came to her profession, she was also immensely generous.

For the first time she was up against one of her own kind, someone with as much ambition, courage, and obstinacy. It was a meeting perhaps not made in heaven, but certainly explosive. Edith the tigress! Edith playing Pygmalion! In love with Montand! Triumphant!

For the first time, not only her voice but her body came alive on stage. Not only did she want the world to know about her love, she also wanted it extolled and celebrated publicly. She would write the lyrics for the celebration of that love that Montand would sing about in public:

She has eyes
Pure as the skies
Hands I adore
More and more
She has smiles
She has wiles
And songs . . .
And she is mine
All mine
Or so I hope . . .[11]

Mine. All mine. Not for very long.

Montand, who was as happy as he was naïve in those early days in Paris, had just been hired by Marcel Carné to play in Carné's new film, *Les Portes de la nuit.* Yves loved his work, the excitement of the film world, and couldn't wait to get back to tell Edith, in minute detail, the events of each day's shooting. Each setup, in fact. She was so bored she wanted to scream.

(Left) Montand had starred in Marcel Carné's film *Les Portes de la Nuit*, and he had been Edith's escort to the opening night of the picture.

(Below) Several years later, Yves and his wife Simone Signoret came to applaud Edith on her opening night.

But the truth lay elsewhere. Piaf the singer had become jealous of Montand the singer. In Lyon, it was he who had scored a triumph. He was blissfully happy and completely unaware of what was happening. Piaf wasn't, though. "When I toured with Yves," she confessed later to René Rouzaud, "he opened the performance and I closed it. He scored triumph after triumph, and night after night I stoically bore my cross."

After an extended tour in Alsace, she returned to Paris with a member of a group known as *Les Compagnons de la Chanson* as her new lover.

Montand was out in the cold, and he didn't know what had hit him. They had laughed together. He admired her. It was the last thing he expected. And perhaps, too, he really loved her. But when that tiny woman made up her mind to do something, nothing could change it. And this time she had made up her mind to play Pygmalion with nine young men, the group who made up Les Compagnons de la Chanson. In the same way she had rid Montand of his American orientation, she was now determined to rid this group of its folklore bent. Piaf always needed to be right.

They lived through the liberation of Paris together.

101

Edith and Les Compagnons de la Chanson, at the Club des Cinq in 1946.

9

LES COMPAGNONS
DE LA CHANSON

Piaf was a lion-tamer.
—Pierre Hiégel

(Above) Edith and one of Les Compagnons de la Chanson, Jean-Louis Jaubert.

(Opposite) One night, in a nightclub in Lausanne, she heard a song that went straight to her heart.

In Piaf's life, there was always Sister Theresa . . . and always a man!

When Piaf left Montand standing on the doormat on the rue de Berri, it was because she had returned from her Alsatian tour with "someone." That someone was Jean-Claude Jaubert, one of Les Compagnons de la Chanson.

The process was always the same with Piaf. She became interested in something because of someone. This time, because she was interested in one member of a group, she became interested in the whole group. Besides, Edith was sufficiently attuned to her own "legend" and to a sense of the comic to know that her public would be delighted to learn that she was in love with nine men at once! Nothing was grand enough for her. Nothing was wild enough! Edith-Bluebeard sought counsel from Sister Theresa. Tell me, Sister, didn't Our Lord have twelve disciples?

It was during the war that she had heard the group sing for the first time. She was struck by their boy-scout purity, and impressed by their talent. She gave them a few pieces of professional advice, none of which they chose to follow. But Piaf was not someone to give up so easily!

One evening, in Lausanne, in a nightclub called Le Coup de Soleil, Edith heard a song that went straight to her heart: *Les Trois Cloches*. The author of the song, Gilles, who was also the owner of the nightclub, gave her an exclusive on it. Edith sensed that it was a song that wouldn't work as a simple solo, so she suggested it to Les Compagnons de la Chanson. Their response was, "Thanks, but no thanks."

"What if I were to sing it with you?" suggested Edith-the-Stubborn.

Les Compagnons de la Chanson couldn't believe their ears. The Great Piaf, sing it *with* them? They immediately sensed that this was an opportunity not to be missed, and began to work on the song together. At first, Piaf simply hummed the tune while the group did the singing. It was a method she would try later with Charles Dumont. Les Compagnons were still not convinced the whole thing was going to work, but one day Jean Cocteau came by to hear them practice, and pronounced the results "sublime." From then on, they were converted.

To sing with them, Piaf for the first time in her career transformed herself physically, and came on stage in a long, pale blue dress. She looked like a little girl all dressed up for her first Communion, lost in a herd of men. Again she had taken one giant step in her search to recover her lost childhood!

The song *Les Trois Cloches—The Three Bells—*was a resounding success, not only in France but throughout the world. In America it came out as *The Song of Jimmy Brown* and went straight up the charts. It sold over a million records worldwide.

Edith's next gift to her group was a song called *La Marie,* written for her by André Grassi. It won France's top prize, *Le Grand Prix du Disque.* Les Compagnons had to admit that their fairy godmother was right, and when she announced that she was going to modernize their repertoire, they didn't even put up a fight.

Edith was delighted with her nine-man team. The year before she had gone to New York and scored an astonishing triumph. She decided to make another trip there, and this time she would take her nine proteges with her.

It was here, in the heart of New York, that the strange love story between Edith and America was to begin.

10
LOVE STORY
WITH AMERICA

The Statue of Liberty, Lafayette, Maurice Chevalier, Dior, perfume and Piaf, all are excellent exports. Governments come and go, but Charlie de Gaulle would always be able to count on this little lady in her black dress, who belongs to the Fifth Republic and those to come after it, as much as the Left Bank does. He should include her in his political family; it would stabilize his regime and help strengthen the franc.   *—Variety*

To be successful in my native France, where people speak the same language and understand me, is nothing: my aim is an international career. I want to make people cry even when they don't understand my words.
   —Edith Piaf

The students at Columbia University asked Piaf to sing *Mon Accordéoniste* in front of the Statue of Liberty. In San Francisco, she passed in review the sailors of the *Jeanne d'Arc.*   *—France-Soir*

It took all of Edith Piaf's great talent to impose on the American public a repertoire so profoundly foreign to the Americans' innate optimism. Not only did she do it, but she provoked reactions such as this from a Jewish reporter in New York after her appearance at Constitution Hall: "With Piaf, it's Yom Kippur every day."   —Henri Pierre,
       Le Monde

Piaf leaving for the United
States, in 1945.

L ike so many of Edith Piaf's loves, her relationship with America began badly.
Throughout her career, Piaf always provoked wildly enthusiastic critical reactions, reviews that were often so irrational
and emotional that they defied analysis. More cantata
than review. "A popular singer who brings back to life
the tragedy of ancient times . . ." "Marvelous Edith,
stunning Edith . . ." "Edith Piaf's songs are the legend of
the centuries . . ." "In her little black dress, like some
dream usherette; her hands alone, sticking to her skirt like
seaweed, express all the sadness of the world."

When Edith, after the Liberation, decided that she
wanted to become an international star and made up
her mind that step one was the conquest of America, it
meant among other things that she had finally come to
terms with the fact that she had bridged the gap between
the slums of Ménilmontant and the gleaming façades of
the Champs-Elysées. She had conquered first France, then Europe. But
that was not enough. With typical generosity, she decided to take along
her Les Compagnons de la Chanson. Very often in her career, Edith, who
in most aspects of her life was a tigress, thought of others before she
thought of herself, and the results were almost always disastrous.

110

Despite all her efforts to update the repertoire of Les Compagnons, and rid them of their folkloric quality, that aspect was precisely what the American public wanted to hear, while Piaf went to lick the wounds caused by her first bitter failure.

In retrospect, her failure is easy to explain, and especially interesting in view of her later conquest of America, due to hard work, intelligence, and persistence.

The fact was, that when Piaf appeared in New York in her little black dress, hands glued to her sides, she represented the exact opposite of the image Americans had built up of French women as "sexy." In addition, they did not understand the words of her songs, and to overcome the problem it had been arranged that a master of ceremonies—an American institution—would present a digest of each song before she sang it, thus diluting its emotional impact. Finally, what the public wanted from her was sparkle and wit, but what she gave them was somber and sad.

Edith and Les Compagnons de la Chanson at the Gare Saint-Lazare, on their way to the train for Le Havre, where they would board ship to the United States. Playing to the crowd come to see them off, they borrow the little baggage cart and ride it to their compartments.

Edith among the sky-
scrapers . . . But America
was not yet ready to re-
ceive the little woman in
black.

The meeting of Ingrid Bergman and Edith Piaf at the Versailles in the Fall of 1948.

Piaf then and there made up her mind that she still would win over that recalcitrant public, even if it meant going home and learning English. She saw her first trip not as a defeat but as a challenge.

She arranged for her American agent to rent for her the most elegant supper club in New York at the time, the Versailles, whose stage was raised for her. And from here she wove the magic spell that won over her American public. Her performances were sold out, and limousines lined the street all along the block of the Versailles, as the wealthy and famous came not only to listen but to kiss her hands, as if she were a goddess, a saint. The Versailles became indissolubly linked with the name and fame of Piaf in America. It was there that the famous not only from the East Coast but also the West, came to hear and applaud her, actors that Edith had till then only admired from afar: Henry Fonda, Orson Welles, Charles Boyer, Judy Garland, Sonja Henie, Bette Davis, Barbara Stanwyck, Dorothy Lamour. And, above all, Marlene, with whom Edith established a strange and beautiful friendship.

It was at the Versailles, too, that she sang the night Marcel Cerdan died. Those who heard her that night say they will never forget it, that they felt as though they were hearing a voice that was coming from beyond the grave. That night, there was also another audience outside the Versailles, a huge throng, religious yet vampirelike, who waited to

115

catch a glimpse of the mourning "Queen Piaf" and say that they had seen her that tragic night.

And it was at the Versailles too, following Cerdan's death, when Edith began to mix tranquilizers and stimulants too often, and when she took to drinking too much beer, that the inevitable downfall came. There were nights when her public, however sympathetic, could not refrain from noticing that a line was slurred, another forgotten, or that, in making her entrance or exit, she seemed to stumble.

Still, her conquest of America was swift and complete, and America was never to forget her.

116

Marlene Dietrich and Jean
Gabin.

11
PIAF AND MARLENE

In the little corner bar
is where
she reigns supreme.
Her flaming head
of hair,
Her mouth a bright red scar
Ah, but her heart, they say,
Her heart is dead.

> —From *At the Sign of
> the Heartless Girl*
> (Words and music
> by Gilles)

Piaf wore around her neck a
little cross encrusted with
emeralds that had been
blessed by the Pope. It was a
gift from Marlene Dietrich.

> —Jacqueline Cartier

Marlene confessed that Piaf's voice had a power of seduction that she had never heard before.

The meeting between Piaf and Marlene was truly a double case of love at first sight.

Marlene came to hear Piaf sing in New York, and the voice of that tiny woman in black touched her and moved her as much as anything she had ever experienced. And Piaf, who during the war had heard that erotically charged, dreamy voice, who had time and again at Billy's put on the record and heard her intone: *Ich bin von Kopf bis fuss* . . . was equally smitten. She had never thought she could experience such a mixture of admiration and feeling for another woman, and yet they fell into each other's arms as though they had been waiting all their lives for this meeting.

Piaf and Marlene . . . Fire and ice . . . The Red and the Black . . . The vamp and the lost little girl. But each a star with a voice capable of moving one to tears.

Marlene was Germany, Piaf was France, and their meeting ground

120

was America. Marlene wanted to forget that she was German, Piaf wanted to forget that she had once been a street urchin: only in New York were such things possible.

The two idols took each other by the hand. Despite all their differences, they resembled each other in some strange way, and that was one of their secrets. Their cruelty was in proportion with their physical makeup. Blond and lovely, Marlene was in her songs the implacable woman with whom men fall madly in love and over whom they eat their hearts out. Piaf, the tiny sparrow, is the woman who has been abandoned, cast aside, mistreated, and whose heart is irreparably broken.

The only song they both sang was *La Vie en rose,* and it is curious that it is a song that resembles neither one of them.

The hidden bond that united them—the magic, intimate link—was that both of them were idolized by soldiers as well as homosexuals.

The story is told that during the war one of Hitler's blond angels

122

followed Piaf everywhere and waited for her virtually every night at the stage door of whatever theater or nightclub where she was performing. He never uttered a word, but when she passed him he would simply kneel down and bow his head.

"Close the door," Edith used to hiss at Andrée Bigard as soon as she was safely in her dressing room. "That guy sends shivers up and down my spine."

As for Marlene, the story goes that she could not bear the ambiguous ardor of the men who claimed they could never love anyone but her.

The fact remains that in every homosexual nightclub in the world, the female trinity that makes it all right for men to dance together are the

Like Piaf, Marlene also sang for the troops during the war.

voices of Marlene, Piaf and Marilyn Monroe. Together they form the three-headed Notre Dame of Homosexuals: Shiva, Vishnu and Krishna. Together they are all the wounds of the world, all the pain and sorrow. If they—their voices—gave soldiers and sailors the strength to die, they also enabled men to accept themselves for what they were, without regard for society's norms. Unhappiness is bearable if ecstasy is possible. And when Piaf's voice rent the silence of their blue night, singing:

> *Don't care what people say*
> *Don't give a damn about their laws*
> *Nothing will ever stand in my way*
> *No one will ever make me stay*
> *Away from the one I love* [12]

it was absolution, exorcism, communion and sharing.

The friendship between Piaf and Marlene was real and without hint of any ambiguity. It was a love more true than the ones that Piaf dreamed up for herself. When Piaf collapsed on stage at Melun, Marlene rushed to her side. At Piaf's funeral, Marlene's face looked for all the world like the Pietà of Avignon.

Piaf wanted to be immortal. Her voice assured her of that, a voice that would haunt the world till the end of time, a voice that would be imitated again and again but never equaled, because hers expressed, as perhaps no one ever had in song, the true sadness and grief of the world.

Her expression is also eternal, as is that extraordinary photograph of Marlene and Piaf together, Marlene in her mink coat, at the height of her beauty, seated next to Piaf, luminous in her plain black dress. Both are looking in the same direction, toward their public, toward life, but also toward death.

With Marlene at her side, Edith knew that she had "arrived," not only as an artist but also as a full-fledged member of society. And that was something she sorely wanted: to be accepted. Like so much about Piaf, it was another of her many contradictions.

124

12
CERDAN

What you do, Edith, is better
than what I do. You bring
them happiness and love.
—Marcel Cerdan

I think you have to pay for
love with bitter tears.
—Edith Piaf

To fully understand the emotion provoked by the Piaf-Cerdan "idyll," one must realize that if Cerdan had not been killed in that plane crash in the Azores, he doubtless would have gone the way of all of Piaf's earlier lovers. It is important to demystify that story immediately, so that it may retain its dreamlike quality, the perfect cliché in Piaf's life, the storybook image of her dark legend. When death overtook him, Piaf had not yet had the time to drop Cerdan, and thus they were fixed for all eternity as star-crossed lovers.

Piaf was alone in New York after her appearance had ended, not in failure but certainly not in triumph. While she had not yet conquered America, Les Compagnons de la Chanson had indeed scored a major triumph and signed a contract to tour all the major cities of America, leaving their "godmother" back in the Big Apple.

But Edith was not languishing in Gotham. She was studying English four hours a day in preparation for her next assault on the city, and whenever Edith was learning she was transfigured, doubtless another throwback to her lost childhood. Her English accent was shaping up nicely; in fact, she had hardly any accent at all. Edith had a gift for

languages, and she refused to sing in any country unless the songs she sang in a foreign language were translated for her. She had done this during the war with Germany, and in that language too her accent was faultless.

One day Cerdan telephoned her. They had met once at the Club des Cinq in Paris. Here they both were in New York, both page-one items for

the American press, so why not get together one evening and have dinner?

Piaf was delighted.

A boxer!

What a pleasant change from her usual crowd.

What she did not know at the time of that call was that that simple,

decent, naïve, uncultured man who talked with his hands, was going to make her heart beat faster than it had probably ever beaten before. The reason was simple: it was the first time in her love life that Edith was not put in a position of being able to help someone professionally. She and Marcel were equals. They admired each other from the very depths of their innocence.

Cerdan was overwhelmed by what he detected behind Edith's voice. She was overcome by the boundless decency of the man.

One night he took her out to Coney Island, where they had a ball on the various rides in the amusement park. They were like two kids. When they got off the scenic railway, the crowd recognized Cerdan and applauded him. Then it recognized Edith, and the cry went up: "Sing us

La Vie en rose!" Piaf had become the image of happiness that she had always believed was destined to elude her.

It was during Cerdan's reign that Edith was invited to the table of Princess Elizabeth—who was not yet Queen of England—and it was then, too, that Charlie Chaplin would break into tears when he heard her sing. If ever there was a period of true happiness in Piaf's life, it was when she was with Marcel, her darling colonial Frenchman who was all good and decent. In her dreams (which were sometimes in English now) she could reach up and touch the sky with her hands—those hands which looked like starfish.

"With Marcel," she told journalist Jean Noli, "I had found my equilibrium. He was so simple and modest and good. We spent our evenings together like an old married couple. He would read his favorite comic strips, laughing out loud at the adventures of Tarzan and Felix the Cat and Mickey Mouse. I'd be knitting a scarf. When we went out together he never swaggered or boasted, though he was the toast of the town. He was incredibly patient with everyone who came up to him and asked for an autograph."

He taught Piaf—who had her moments of irritation when faced with crowds—to respect these people. "After all," he would say, "they're the ones who have made you famous."

Still, she could not contain her Pygmalion instincts, and before long she began to make Cerdan read literature rather than his beloved comic strips. One day in New York, Michel Emer, who wrote more than twenty-six songs for Piaf, arrived to find Cerdan terribly distressed. He was holding a copy of Gide's *L'Immoraliste* in his hand.

"Listen, Michel," he said painfully, "would you mind telling me something? This guy Gide, is it possible he's a little gay?"

Marcel's manager, Lucien Roupp, was not exactly overjoyed about Marcel's amorous adventure with Piaf: it was the first time his protegé had escaped him.

Edith, though, was in seventh heaven. She had become the "wife," which made her enormously happy. To be sure, her conscience did bother her whenever she thought of Marcel's real wife, Marinette, and their children, but she didn't mean anyone any harm, she kept telling herself. And besides, there was nothing she could do about it. Marcel was her destiny.

Actually, it was she who became his destiny, by asking Marcel to move up his return trip to New York. He did, and the plane he was on crashed in the Azores, killing everyone on board, including the superb French violinist Ginette Neveu.

Without question, Cerdan's death was the heaviest blow Piaf had to endure in a life that was rarely easy. It marked the beginning of her

Cerdan to Michel Emer, after reading one of Gide's novels at Edith's behest: "Listen, Michel, would you mind telling me something? This guy Gide, is it possible he's a little gay?"

decline, of the period when she fell completely apart. It was as though all the misfortunes that she had sung about had become reality, as though song and life had suddenly become one.

Up to now, it was she who had provoked the daily dramas, the scenes and break-ups that were part and parcel of her life. She needed them in order to live, as material for her songs: they were her daily bread.

After Cerdan's death, her madness—what one might term her divine madness—which heretofore had led her toward life, now led her ineluctably toward death.

When on that fateful day in October 1949 Cerdan's plane went down in the Azores, Piaf had fourteen more years to live. Fourteen years that she was going to devour the way she had devoured her childhood, that she was going to slash at in the same way life had slashed her.

Edith was invited to the table of Princess Elizabeth, the future Queen of England.

When *France-Dimanche* suggested that she write a series of articles for them about her life, for the then astronomical price of $2,000 an article, and when Piaf accepted because as usual she was broke, she mentioned to Jean Noli, who was the coauthor of the articles, "Tell your boss that I don't want a penny for the article dedicated to Cerdan." That series of confessions, as they were called, increased the circulation of the newspaper by 300,000 copies!

The same condition obtained when Charles Dumont wrote the music for a song entitled *La belle histoire d'amour,* the words of which Edith herself had written:

> *When a man comes toward me*
> *I go toward him*
> *Toward I'm not sure what*
> *I walk in the night* [13]

"Listen, Charles," she said to him, "I want it understood that I don't want to touch a penny for that song, which I wrote in memory of Marcel." Her accounting was always beyond words: God, Love, Money.

After Cerdan, Piaf's loves were to become diabolical and sometimes downright shabby. She would force love's hand with that same destructive sense she so often displayed. She would "manufacture" singers in the same way she might have given birth to the children she never had. Moustaki was the only one among them whose talent was real, but even he was a flash in the pan. The others were not even serious enough to be considered.

Edith and Marcel Cerdan went to Coney Island to have a good time. The crowd recognized Edith and made her sing *La Vie en rose.*

137

Ginette Neveu.

13
THE OUIJA BOARD

| Death is the beginning of something. —Edith Piaf | Death does not exist. —Edith Piaf |

Piaf at the wedding of Robert and Monique Chauvigny.

The story of the Ouija board is a sad and sorry one.

The mother of Ginette Neveu, the concert violinist who died in the plane crash that killed Cerdan, called Edith one day to tell her that she had succeeded in communicating with her daughter beyond the grave.

From that time on, Edith was obsessed with the idea of communicating with Marcel. The surest way, Ginette Neveu's mother assured her, was through an Ouija board. Edith had one bought for her immediately, and as soon as it arrived she put it to use, with sometimes staggering results.

In her present vulnerability, where her pain and sadness were tinged with feelings of tremendous guilt about her role in Cerdan's death, the Ouija board could make her do virtually anything.

140

Those around her were immediately divided into two camps: those who could make the Ouija board work, and those who could not—or who, more accurately, refused to.

The Ouija board was very tough with Edith. It blamed her for her stinginess. It gave her investment advice that almost always redounded to the benefit of the same people who had needled her, through the board, for being niggardly.

Momone, who during the whole Cerdan love affair had been more or less shunted aside, reappeared once again, more powerful than ever. If Edith had avoided her when she was with Marcel, it was because she knew that throughout the years Momone had always tried to steal her lovers when Edith's back was turned.

Now Edith only lived for the hours she could spend bent over the Ouija board. She took it with her wherever she went. Woe to the person who had the misfortune to leave it behind!

Andrée Bigard, who was sickened and disgusted by this new turn of events, consciously "forgot" the board on one of Edith's trips to New York. "Edith," she said, "I'm terribly sorry, but in the haste of our departure I left it behind." Aznavour, who was part of the group, looked down at his feet, afraid to meet Edith's blazing eyes. The rest of the troupe hardly dared breathe.

Edith, livid, ordered Andrée and one of her musicians, Chauvigny, to go straight to Bloomingdale's as soon as they arrived and buy a new board. But however the new board moved to the advantage of others, as far as contact with Cerdan was concerned the results were total failure: Marcel remained silent. At one point Edith was so distraught that she locked Andrée Bigard in her hotel room for twelve days, trying to starve her into submission. Chauvigny used to sneak food up to her. Finally, Edith shipped both Bigard and Aznavour back to Paris, and called for Momone to take the first plane to New York. As soon as Momone arrived, the board began to dance again.

The Ouija board marked the first stop on Piaf's descent into hell.

14
BLACK WEDDING

The first of every month, she took a brand new notebook and wrote in it: "Today a new life begins."
—Lou Barrier

Casablanca, where Piaf went to see Cerdan's widow.

Despite her tendency to play Pygmalion, there is no record that she ever helped another woman. And with one exception— Marguerite Monnot, shown at Piaf's right, above—she never really had a woman friend.

Piaf was a romantic on the one hand, a hooligan on the other. When very young she had dreamed of marrying Paul Meurisse, but it was Michèle Alfa he ended up with. She became the "home-wrecker" that she had always really been, flailing away against established couples as Don Quixote had against windmills. She detested the status quo, the Establishment in all its manifestations. She could only make fun of it, to ridicule, all those things she had never had.

What she hated most of all were the pictures of conventional bliss, especially men who at the end of the day went home to their wife and children.

(Above) Marinette Cerdan, flanked by her sister and Andrée Bigard.

(Below) Piaf with the Cerdan children.

And as for me
I'm like the sea.
My heart's too big
For any single man
And that is why
I write my love
On earth below
On sky above.[14]

The only love she could sing about was love under siege or threat. And suddenly, as a first sacrament, she found herself widowed without ever having been married.

I want to forget you
I can't even start.
The first day I met you
You left with my heart
Then you left me
Bereft . . .[15]

The first real ceremony for Piaf was this funeral-wedding. She was Cerdan's widow: the role fit her to a T. As her bridal head-dress, she wore the black widow's veil.

But there were also Cerdan's legal wife, Marinette, not to mention the Cerdan children.

After having prayed for Marcel and having gone to mass every morning for months on end in the same church where years later she would marry Jacques Pills, Piaf became obsessed with the idea that she had to meet and get to know Marinette and the children. Was it the shopgirl in her wanting to making amends, or the whore wanting to exorcise her guilt? In any case, as soon as she could carve three days out of her schedule, she would go to Casablanca to meet the Cerdan family. A voyage of atonement and domination.

She arrived there her arms full of lavish gifts for everyone. Little Marcel Jr. was nine years old. He hated Edith. She wasn't even aware of his feelings. True to form, she had an idea in mind, and she intended to follow it through. Now it was no longer the Ouija board dictating her actions, but a combination of Sister Theresa, Jesus, and the "law of the underworld."

Marinette, the wife that Cerdan had never paraded in public; Marinette, the dutiful, submissive, Mediterranean wife, was dazzled by the visit of "Queen Piaf."

Parenthetically, it should be noted that Edith, no matter how strong her impulse to reshape people and restructure their lives, had never helped another woman. Aside from the composer Marguerite Monnot, Piaf never had a true female friend, and she never helped advance the career of any other woman. Her misogyny was such that when performing anywhere she never asked the usherettes what they thought of her performance; she only asked for the opinion of the men who worked backstage.

But here she was nonetheless ready to take care of Marinette, for in the context of her personal accountability—God, money, and love—Edith understood that she had a debt to pay to Marinette and Cerdan's children. She talked Marinette into bringing the children with her to Boulogne, to that same house where she and Marcel had lived together. There she would provide for them, take care of them, make sure they had everything they wanted and needed. She would exorcise the demon.

Marinette accepted, and two months later she arrived.

Edith had laid out on her "rival's" bed a fur coat. A magnificent fur coat.

Edith was "giving back" to Marinette the coat that Marcel had given her.

Piaf took Marinette to all the leading dressmakers in Paris.

Edith dressed Marinette in the finest clothes; she personally arranged her hair; she made her up in the latest fashion. She introduced her to all the famous people in Paris.

What was the outcome of all this attention? It was, inevitably, the unexpected. Or perhaps, the expected. As it turned out, what fascinated Marinette much more than all the wealth and material goods that Edith lavished upon her were the lovers she seemed to draw like moths to a light. The more one studies Piaf's life, the clearer it becomes that Piaf always aroused in other women this feeling both of identification and of rivalry. Other women always wanted what Piaf had, and Piaf always wanted other women's men.

Whether she was Christian or pagan, saint (!) or sinner, Piaf always enjoyed herself. In this instance, she managed to transform her adultery into a large family.

But a few months after the Cerdans arrived in Paris, Edith sold this house where she had been happy, first with Marcel, then with his family. She not only sold it, but sold it at a considerable loss. Why? She couldn't bear to live there any more.

(Right) The bicycle racer Toto Gérardin.

(Below) A note left by Piaf for Andrée Bigard: "Don't wake me up unless Toto calls, in which case put him right through. I can't bear not hearing from him any longer. Love and kisses, E." The note on page 150 says much the same thing.

15
THE YEAR OF
THE BICYCLE

He was slim, seductive, and
his sad expression drew me
to him: he was a champion
bicycle racer.
—*France-Dimanche*

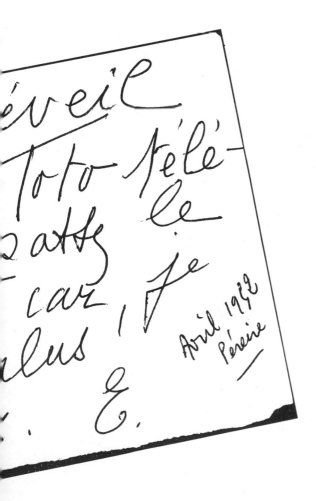

Dé

<u>En dehors de Toto</u>
nous ne sommes là
pour personne,
qu'on nous laisse
dormir jusqu'à
plus soif !

Les deux
orphelines

After Cerdan's death, it was not so much bad luck that befell her as disorder and chaos. It was a time of accidents, sickness, tranquilizers, and drugs.

It was as though she had lost her center of gravity, and no one could keep her from her precipitous, downhill slide. She continued to go through the motions, but it was clear her heart wasn't in it.

She became more demanding than ever, but even that rang hollow. Aznavour suffered more than anyone: she constantly gave him a hard time, turning down his songs and in general persecuting him any way she could—even though he was one of the rare colleagues with whom she did not have an affair. Aznavour, in fact, was one of the few professional errors Edith ever made. She completely misjudged him as a composer. Thus she turned down his *Gloomy Sunday,* which he had written especially for her, and which Juliette Gréco eventually sang with enormous success worldwide. Perhaps the problem was that Piaf and Aznavour were too much alike. Yet despite all this, Aznavour was one of the few people who, in the waning years of her life, would help her.

There followed in rapid succession a series of men. First among them was an ungainly American, Eddie Constantine, who came to see her in Paris one day. At that time, 1951, Edith was preparing to act in Marcel Achard's *La Petite Lilli,* which was directed by the prestigious Raymond

(*Opposite*) Extract from a letter dated March 8, 1953, to Andrée Bigard, written from New York at nine in the morning: "I need a long rest, I don't sleep any more and I'm really at the end of my nerves. In Miami I had to stop the show twice and couldn't go on, a case of overall fatigue. I honestly have to have some rest. Toto drove me almost crazy, and the medicine I was taking for my rheumatism didn't help matters, either...."

151

une grande détente, j'ai besoin d'
dormir plus et suis dans un état
de nerf indescriptible, ici à
Miami, j'ai arrêté mon
tour deux fois en -plein milieu
sans pouvoir reprendre, une
fatigue générale, j'ai besoin
vraiment d'un grand repos,
Toto m'a détraqué tout mes
nerfs et le traitement aux
anti-rhumatismes m'a rien arran-
gé,

Rouleau. The producer was Mitty Goldin, never a Piaf fan from the start and who, despite her meteoric career, had only agreed to produce the play at the A.B.C. Theater after a lot of arm-twisting. Piaf not only convinced him to do it but made him take on Eddie Constantine as her costar. The play lasted seven months—precisely the length of their love affair. After which Constantine went back to his wife and daughter.

Edith replaced him with a bicycle racer named André Pousse, who later on went into movies. He couldn't get over her: when he came home at night she would kneel down and put on his slippers. "Jesus!" he would exclaim later, in telling the tale, "after all it wasn't my *maid* doing it, it

Eddie Constantine, Piaf, and Aznavour performing in 1951.

153

& je vous embrasse bien
et suis folle de joie de
vous voir!

Votre petite fille
Votre enfant terrible,
mais qui vous aime   Edith

C'est sinistre dans la
maison ici...—tout le monde
dors; pourquoi Dieu du
ciel je ne peux pas arriver
a dormir?

Vivement Dimanche, j'ai le
mal de Paris et de tous
ceux que j'aime!

Que chacun fasse a son
idée!

was *Edith Piaf!*" He beat her not because she was unfaithful to him, but because he found her maddening and exasperating. She kept him on such a short leash that he couldn't train any longer. She decided she would sell her country house and buy him a car. She decided he ought to play opposite her in *Le Bel Indifférent*. She decided . . . She decided. He couldn't take it any more and left.

His replacement was another bicycle racer, Toto Gérardin. With this one we move from near tragedy to pure vaudeville again. Gérardin's wife hired a private detective to follow her husband, and the easy trail led straight to Edith's, where he found not only an imposing number of gold and silver trophies that Toto had won, but a mink coat and eighteen gold bars—all presumably presents from Toto to Edith. Not in Mrs. Gérardin's eyes, they weren't, and before you could say "Piaf" they were all safe and sound back home where they belonged.

Following the "Year of the Bicycle," Edith spiraled further downward into what can only be called the "Cycle of Automobile Accidents," which was the real beginning of her physical downfall. In quick succession, she had two bad accidents while driving with Charles Aznavour. They were the results, no doubt, of the diabolical rhythm she imposed on her friends and colleagues: stay up all night talking, then leave at dawn for the next town where she was to sing that night, in time to rehearse and check the lighting before the performance. She broke several ribs, had her arm in a cast. The pain was more than she could bear. To ease it, there were a couple of choices: drugs or alcohol. Why choose one when you could have both? The downward spiral continued.

(Opposite) From Piaf to Bigard: "I kiss you, Dée, and can't wait to see you. Your little girl, your *enfant terrible,* who nonetheless loves you a lot. There's something sinister about the house here. . . . Everyone sleeps like a log, so why in God's name can't I? I can't tell you how much I miss Paris and everyone there I love! P. S. Tell Chang to do whatever he wants!"

(Below) On September 7, 1958, Edith completely wrecked her automobile, pictured here in the garage after the accident in Dreux. How she escaped alive is anyone's guess.

16
THE BLUE WEDDING: JACQUES PILLS

Why did they leave her? Because she wore you out by forcing you to adapt to her own crazy lifestyle: she used to go to bed at eight in the morning. No one could keep up with her. Either they divorced her or they became neurasthenic. Jacques Pills almost had a nervous breakdown. When they were with her, even the hardiest athletes became no more than a shadow of their former selves at the end of six months.

—Michel Rivgauche

(*Opposite*) Edith and her husband, Jacques Pills.

Piaf, who thought of herself as Cerdan's widow, still had not married. Increasingly, she dreamed of a marriage ceremony the way, as a little girl, she had dreamed of the first Communion she never had. Jacques Pills, a tall, handsome and famous singer, would be not only her next lover but her official husband, too. At the time she married him, she was already fairly far gone on drugs, and the self-destruction was growing steeper.

She married him in New York, in September 1952, in the same church where she used to go and pray every day for the peace of Marcel Cerdan's soul.

She got married in a pale blue dress (the color of Les Compagnons de la Chanson), and Marlene Dietrich was her witness. Radiant, drugged,

she hoped against hope that her "image" would be stronger than she.

She sang at the Versailles, he at La Vie en Rose. Their honeymoon was spent in endless taxi rides across Manhattan from one nightclub to the other.

Pills was a sweet and decent man. In other words, weak. Edith gobbled him up in one bite. She longed for the good old days filled with fun and frolic, the silliness she remembered when she was a little girl. She knew he was jealous, so she played little tricks, such as sitting through three showings of a film so that when she finally got home Jacques would be convinced she had been out with another man . . . and therefore would beat her. But Pills was not the beating kind: he was a sheep in sheep's clothing. Perhaps what most amused Piaf—who thought of all other

159

women, especially if they were famous or attractive, as her rivals—about their relationship was that Pills had once been married to the French singer Lucienne Boyer, who had been the toast of Paris when Edith started at Leplée's. She could still remember Lucienne singing *Parlez-moi d'amour* in a cabaret on the Avenue Junot, and how all Paris was at her feet.

The happiness of the Ducos—for that was Pills' real name—boils down to a few songs and a few photographs. Period. Among his hits were the memorable *Je t'ai dans la peau* for which he wrote the lyrics and Gilbert Bécaud the music.

Once again Piaf was devouring life as though she were starving, but this time, like Little Red Riding Hood, she would be devoured, herself.

Piaf and Georges Mous-
taki at Maxim's in 1958.

17

THE MYSTIC AND HELL
THE GREEK AND
THE AMERICAN

Your songs filled with
sunshine, with wild girls,
with passionate love, will
take you a long way.
                —Piaf to Moustaki

Piaf died because she was
bored.   —Moustaki

She was an extraordinary
patient. Her sickness was
solitude. Her obsession: the
fear of being alone. So she
surrounded herself with a
group of people who amused
and distracted her. To
become a Piaf groupie, you
had to know how to make
her laugh, arouse her
curiosity, or excite her about
a subject she knew little
about. As a result her meals
were crazy: a gangster, a
bum, two boxers, and Jean
Cocteau. —Michel Rivgauche

It's absolutely crazy. She's
killing everyone by the
totally chaotic life she leads.
All the people around her
are on their knees. Even her
doctor.   —Douglas Davies

She was a woman who rose
from the most humble
origins. Nothing she ever did
really affected that. She
integrated the people into
her every emotion.
                    —Moustaki

When Moustaki first met Piaf in 1957, he was struck by her loneliness, but he was not in the least interested in her either as a woman or a singer. That didn't bother Piaf: whether she wanted a song or a man, other people's feelings never deterred her. Moustaki had written *Milord*, a song she greatly admired. He would become her guitarist. It was really quite simple. As it turned out, it was far from that: it was demonic. Moustaki had far too much personality, was too much the Greek "macho" to let himself be dominated by her or anyone. He also found her lifestyle absolutely scandalous. He refused to put up with her silly little games and disapproved of her hangers-on. What he did respect in her was her professionalism, her dedication to her work and art, but he was not about to let that admiration blind him to the realities of what she was, even if she showered him with presents in the hope that he would reciprocate and shower her with black-and-blue marks.

They were lovers for a short while, then he dropped her—just the way she tells it in so many of her songs. When he did, she was in an American hospital. He had drained the cup to its dregs. Edith and her groupies called him every name in the book, and a few that were not, but in truth he was disgusted to see her so-called friends all too willing to supply her not only with alcohol but drugs as well, while others pushed her further and further into the frenzy of mysticism.

Meanwhile, Edith continued her endless round of "games"—some conscious, others meant no doubt to draw attention to herself. Her friend Lou Barrier tired of finding her all puffy and barely conscious. "What happened, Edith? What happened?" he one day implored, beside himself with worry. She pointed vaguely under the bed. He stooped down only to discover there twenty empty beer cans.

One of Edith's groupies at the time was Doug Davies, a handsome young American painter. Each day he made a pilgrimage to Edith's to

ask how she was and bring a small bouquet of flowers. A light went on in Lou Barrier's head. What Edith needed was a new "love." He knew full well he was sending Doug into the lion's den without a sword. He introduced them. For Edith it was love at first sight. Doug soon became Edith's lover. And once again, with a new love to focus on, Edith willed herself back to life and health. What she failed to understand was that he was not so much in love with her as

Piaf and Doug Davies.

with her image: Edith-as-Singer. But she would vamp him as she had so many others. She took him back to France with her.

I kissed him for the first time the afternoon he arrived holding five colored balloons floating on the end of their little strings, she would write. To Lou Barrier she confided: "As for that other son-of-a-bitch, I can't even remember who he was." Moustaki was dead and gone.

Perhaps Edith needed to rid herself of the previous lover before she could love again, but Doug wasn't bothered by the knowledge of his predecessors. Unlike Moustaki, he was not overly bothered by the hangers-on, but fit right in. For them, he simply became the New Boss. If some of their shenanigans did upset him, his protests lacked conviction.

For the love of Doug, Edith, who couldn't swim a stroke, took lessons.

Like a faithful puppy, he followed Edith wherever she went on tour. Not that their life was a bed of roses: they fought like cats and dogs, but then when did Edith not? He painted a series of harrowing pictures of her, and she as usual showered her lover with gifts. But at the thirtieth easel she had given him, he flew into a rage. The lady's absolutely crazy!

She took him to the Riviera, where things improved. Doug loved the sea, and felt more at home there. The French watched the curious couple with amazement, their tiny idol, dressed in a sailor suit—the same person they were paying a fortune to hear sing that night—on the arm of her young American. Edith was aggressive and an exhibitionist, but to all appearances she seemed to be blissfully happy, contrary to the conventional image they had of her.

Her tour, according to the lyricist Michel Rivgauche, was totally mad. He wrote several of the songs that she sang during this period—*La Foule, Faut pas qu'il se figure, Salle d'attente, Mon vieux Lucien*—and the sublime *Blouses blanches* which Coquatrix judged to be unsingable. When he said as much to Edith, she retorted, "But you know as well as I do, people say that I could sing the phone book and make it sound good."

Piaf sang in Cannes to great acclaim and indulged her culinary whims. She devoured the cheeses sprinkled with southern herbs, and made the chef smother hers with chives. When she had melon with port, she made the maître d' literally inundate the melon with wine. "Why be so stingy?" she admonished him. "After all, you're not paying for it!"

In the south, Piaf took swimming lessons. Why? Because Doug was a swimmer. Some things changed in Edith's life, but there was one constant: if she was with a swimmer, she took swimming lessons; if she was with a boxer, she talked boxing incessantly; if her lover of the moment was Greek, she became passionately interested in Greek history.

Doug lasted a few months, then turned tail and ran for his life. Edith fell ill, was rushed to the hospital, and operated on for inflammation of the pancreas. She remained hospitalized until October 1959. A doctor who treated her at the time attests that, physiologically speaking, she was already dead. She had been, he asserted, for several years, in fact!

Be that as it may, the entire population of France was able to witness her resurrection, and the recordings of the three recitals she gave at the Olympia in 1960, 1961, and 1962 are the diamonds of the final, hopeless love affair between Piaf and her public. A public which, as much as the medical concoctions urged upon her to enable her to go on stage, kept her going, and singing, during those final years.

(Opposite) Doug Davies, Piaf, and Coquatrix in 1958.

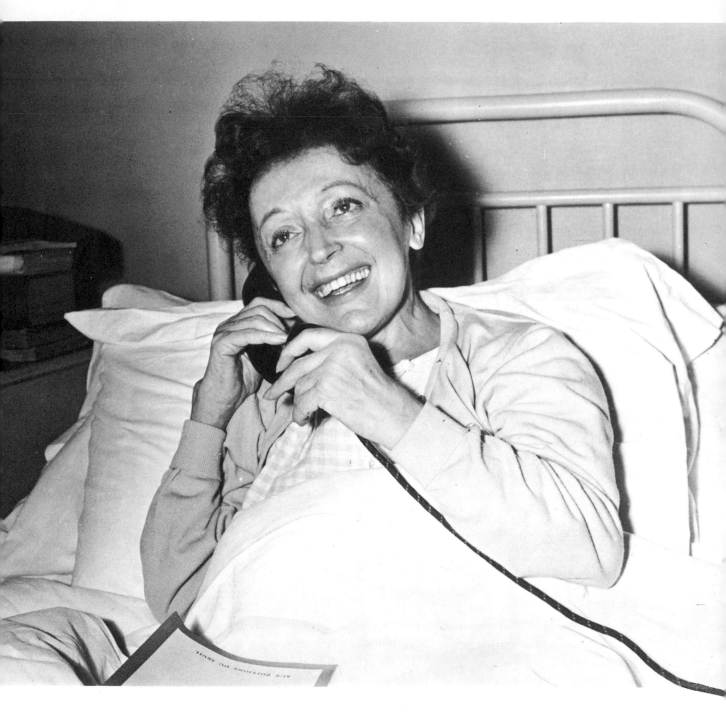

The latter part of Edith's life was spent recovering from the illnesses and accidents that plagued it. Still, even bed-ridden, the magic smile was almost always there.

18
CALVARY

About five hundred yards before we reached our destination, the automobile seemed to leave the ground and skidded out of control. A tire had just blown out. We staggered into a bar, which turned out to be the same bar where we had had a post-performance party several months earlier. Now, though, we were bloodied and battered. The people thought they were seeing ghosts.

   —Moustaki, in an interview about the accident he and Edith were in

If I weren't burning myself out, do you think I'd be able to sing?   —Edith Piaf

There were not only accidents. There were also operations: the bleeding ulcer, the intestinal occlusion, the stomach operations, and the hepatic comas.

This calvary was the result of Edith's excesses, despite her heredity (Papa Gassion had always downed ten Pernods before the stroke of noon, day in and day out), Edith had an iron constitution. But before she began using morphine—which she only used when the pain was so atrocious that she was virtually incapable of singing—she had abused her body through the immoderate use of coffee,

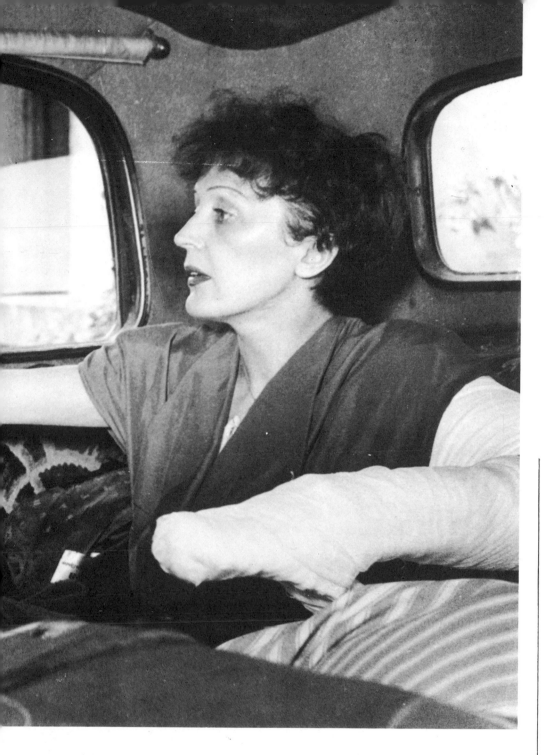

Edith, her left arm in a cast, her right hand being kissed by the singer Roland Avellys. What her relationship with him was can be inferred from the letter on the following page, written to Henri Contet a few months after this photograph, from Washington, D.C. Among other things she warns: "If by chance you should run into Roland Avellys, beware of him, and above all don't lend him any money, either in my name or in yours, for if you do you'll never see it again! I'm trying diplomatically to turn him out of my house, but it's not easy because it goes without saying that he's privy to certain things and doesn't hesitate to use them. Lovely fellow, eh? It serves me right: I'm the only one who still believes in Santa Claus!"

aspirin, and wine, not to mention the indiscriminate popping of uppers and downers whenever she was convinced that one or the other would meet her immediate needs.

When her doctor would prescribe a certain dose of some medicine, she thought nothing of multiplying it by ten or a dozen. After her stomach operation at the American Hospital, in 1959, she had no difficulty in convincing the nurse that the doctor had told her it was all right for her to eat steak au poivre that same evening.

And in the drug department, it was but an easy step to move from

(Opposite) Edith playing *boccie*—or bowls—with, from left to right, Michel Emer, Charles Aznavour, Micheline Dax, and the aforementioned Roland Avellys.

moderate pain killers to heavier, and more dangerous, drugs. She knew she could always find someone—be it a hood, some poor guy interested in making a few hundred francs, or simply one of her slaves—to go out and find her whatever drug she wanted. At the end of her life, when she was practically incapable of even getting up on stage, she had to have an injection in order to sing. Better that than stop, right? The show must go on. Her public was waiting. Edith, who wanted to live two lives at the same time, was destroying herself, not slowly, but swiftly and surely, without discrimination.

HOTEL Statler WASHINGTON

car j'en ai besoin! Et toi! Que fais tu? Tu vas probablement partir en vacances aussi? Si parfois tu vois Roland Avellys, méfie toi de lui et surtout ne lui prête rien ni en mon nom ni au sien car tu ne reverrais jamais rien, j'essaie avec diplomatie de le virer de chez moi car évidemment il est au courant de certaines choses et il en profite, joli monsieur, c'est bien fait pour moi, je suis toujours la seule a croire au Père Noël! je ressors toujours de ces histoires découragée et bien triste, c'est la vie, tu fais du bien au gens et tu t'en fais des ennemis! Comment va Charlotte? Embrasse la

Piaf and Charles Dumont,
after a night on the town.

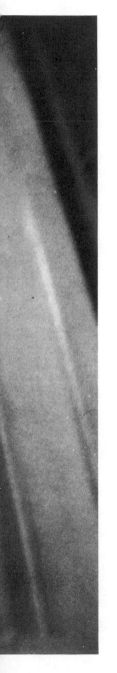

19
RESURRECTION VIA DUMONT

Piaf the Immortal.
—*Les Lettres Françaises*

Fortunately, Edith Piaf is not dead, either for science or song. It is an apotheosis.
—*Arts*

When the spotlights burn or stain the pale and puny wonder-woman with blood, when her pale hands beat the air as though in search of the proper gestures, when her suddenly swelling voice drinks in like a fatal potion the full silence of the auditorium, we give up, bound hand and foot, completely happy to be thus imprisoned.
—Christine de Rivoyre,
Le Monde

Piaf had made up her mind to save the Olympia Theater as Joan of Arc had saved France. The only problem was, she no longer had the strength to do it. Around her, haggard, were gathered several of the Old Faithful: her musician Chauvigny, who was destined to outlive her by only three months; the ineffable Marguerite Monnot, who would die two years before her; the Bonels; and Bruno Coquatrix, who was looking to Edith for his salvation.

She dragged herself around her apartment on the Boulevard Lannes, dressed in her old, unwashed dressing gown, her blue eyes lusterless. Her gait was that of an old woman, and often she would stumble and almost fall. Her impresario, Lou Barrier, was pale and wan. He adored Edith. He was the most generous producer the world of popular music has ever known. For months it had been he who had kept the whole thing going. A combination of Edith's illnesses, her craziness, and her endless string of hangers-on, had resulted in her going more and more deeply into debt.

One day Edith told Coquatrix that despite all her hopes she would have to give up the idea of saving the Olympia. He was devastated by the news, but in his heart of hearts he knew she had tried to do the impossible.

The next day, her friend Michel Vaucaire arrived with a young composer in tow named Charles Dumont. She took an instant dislike to him, but she was too much a professional to let her likes and dislikes affect her career. The song they were bringing her was called *Non, je ne regrette rien*. It was that song that enabled Edith to rise from the ashes of her past. As for young Dumont, it would bring him instant fame and fortune, but his involvement with Edith would cost him his health.

He couldn't believe his ears. The Great Piaf would really take on his song? Before he met her, he was a quiet young man, happily married, with two children. Even dying, Piaf was still capable of "straightening out" that situation! Thus did Dumont witness, through his song, not only the rebirth of perhaps the biggest star the music hall had ever seen, at least in our time, but the apocalypse as well, for as soon as she was back on her feet again, as soon as she had regained some of her strength, she immediately resumed her role of pitiless tyrant.

On December 29, 1960, Edith appeared at the Olympia, with Dumont's song contributing largely to her overwhelming comeback triumph. A half an hour after her performance, the audience was still on its feet, applauding. And the next morning the newspaper headlines in Paris proclaimed:

PIAF RESUSCITATED BY LOVE

Piaf and Charles Dumont at the opening night of Edith's performance at the Olympia, on December 29, 1960.

On tour in 1960, on the comeback trail. Here she is in Rennes, being helped with her coat by Charles Dumont. Bruno Coquatrix is on her left.

Because of that story, the Sunday paper *France-Dimanche* doubled its normal print run. (Three years later, when she died, it would triple its printing.) But her fans were not without their ghoulish side. "If she were to die right there on stage before our very eyes," one was reported to have said, "what a beautiful story to be able to tell our grandchildren!" What they didn't know, of course, was that as soon as the curtain fell, that same little disjointed doll who had torn their hearts out with her songs, who had left them limp and sometimes crying, was taken back-stage and stuffed with vitamins and injected with drugs to keep her going.

Somewhere, though, Edith found the strength and fortitude to go off on another tour. She took Dumont with her. In order to keep going, she downed pills by the handful. Mountains of them. Not without effect: more than once she collapsed on stage. Often she would forget the words to her songs, and even entire songs. And whenever she did she would ask forgiveness of her adoring public. Whenever she fell, she would be helped back onto her feet, and the show would go on. It was frightful.

Piaf had some idea—however vague—of the Goya-like quality she often must have presented to her audiences. But true to herself, as she had been an exhibitionist when it came to love and poverty, so she was

180

the living incarnation of death. With a kind of morbid pleasure, she seemed intent on showing just how far she could push herself.

By this time, young Dumont was on the verge of a nervous breakdown. He suggested that he and Edith go off to the mountains for some winter sports. The poor fellow didn't know what he was saying: making such a suggestion to Edith was like signing his death warrant. To suggest putting Piaf and Mother Nature together was an act of total madness. When Piaf refused to go, he went off by himself. He was excommunicated on the spot. No matter: one of Edith's groupies, Claude Figus, who would go to almost any lengths to please Edith—once he went so far as to fry an egg over the eternal flame of the Arch of Triumph to amuse her—had someone waiting in the wings.

Figus was a sad and curious case. In one sense, he was the lowest of the low of Edith's inner circle, a slave who would stoop to anything to please her, including procuring the drugs he had to know were going to kill her. His excuse—or perhaps his reason—was that he had been hopelessly in love with Piaf since the age of thirteen. For years he tried to be the life of Edith's party, but in the end he paid the price for all the forced hilarity: he killed himself.

Poor Dumont had made the awful mistake of suggesting they go off to winter sports together.

20
THE SECOND GREEK: AN ANGEL

She thought her life belonged to the public, and that her public had the right to know everything, down to the most minute details.
—Théo Sarapo

The "angel" Théo helps Edith during her last days

The young man that Figus had been keeping in the wings for Edith was a sweet, sensitive Greek. His parents owned a hairdressing parlor in the suburbs of Paris. When they first met, Edith found him a trifle on the chubby side. Later on she would put him on a diet. His real name was Théo. She would dub him Sarapo, which she learned was Greek for "I love you." She would make a singer out of him. The last one she would shape and launch. He was an angel with her. She would make a martyr of him.

For a brief time, she would play at being happy. She gave him an electric train. He gave her a stuffed teddy bear bigger than she.*

* The stuffed bear still exists, and is part of the collection on display at the Club des Amis d'Edith Piaf, located at 5, rue Crépin-du-Gast, in Ménilmontant, a stone's throw from where Edith used to sing in the streets as a child.

When Sarapo came into her life, Edith did not want to be drugged with medication again. With all her remaining strength, she threw herself into the task of teaching him to sing. To show her public how far she would go to help him, she appeared with him on the stage of the Bobino. Together they sang *A quoi ça sert l'amour (What Good Is Love)*. She was a walking corpse; he was bare-chested.

Edith's journalist friends, especially those of *France-Dimanche,* were harried by their editor, who used to lament that after Piaf was gone, there would be no more real stars around. They don't make them like her any more, he would sigh.

Edith knew that her real lover—her public—was divided about her relationship with Théo, and so she dreamed up the idea of asking for a public-opinion poll on the subject. The newspaper was only too happy to

The crowd outside the Town Hall of the 16th *Arrondissement* in Paris the day of Edith's wedding to Théo Sarapo.

185

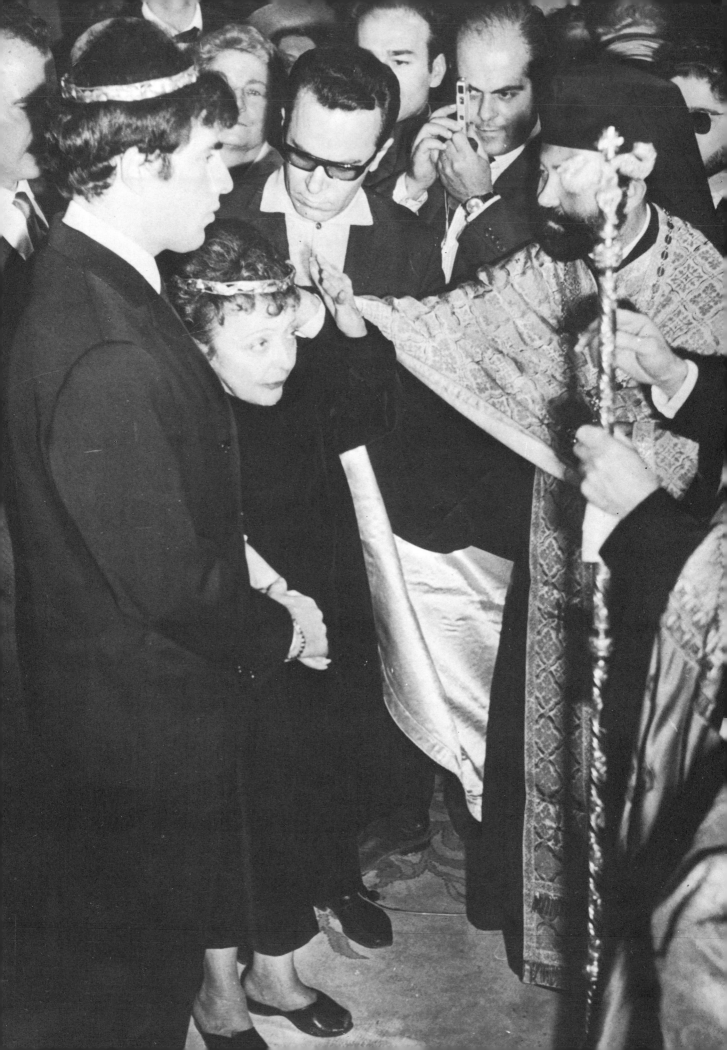

oblige, but it had no idea the reaction it would provoke: thousands upon thousands of letters poured into the *France-Dimanche* offices, overwhelmingly in favor of the liaison. Once again, Edith had been given the absolution she desired. Only in one section of France—Brittany—did the sales of her records show any sign of declining.

One day the photo-journalist Hugues Vassal, who always accompanied Jean Noli on his frequent interviews with Piaf, and had begun to adore her, piped up in the midst of a crowded newspaper editorial meeting:

"What if they were to get married?"

"Who are you talking about?" said one of the editors.

"Edith and Théo. What if she were to marry him?"

The editor-in-chief looked up from his sheaf of papers. "That," he said excitedly, "is an absolutely brilliant idea!"

He ordered Noli and Vassal to Edith's apartment, and told them not to return until they had a paper signed by Edith confirming her intentions to marry Sarapo. *France-Dimanche*, of course, would have the exclusive rights to the story.

Edith found the idea intriguing. Even on death's doorstep, she had

(Above) Théo and Edith waving to the crowds from the balcony, after the ceremony.

(Opposite) The Greek Orthodox ceremony, on October 9, 1962.

187

Piaf bought an electric train for Théo.

always dreamed of incense and wedding bells. With her arthritic hand so twisted with pain she could hardly hold a pen, Edith wrote out for her pals:

EDITH PIAF ANNOUNCES HER FORTHCOMING MARRIAGE TO
THEO SARAPO THIS OCTOBER

"There," she said, handing the paper to them. "I hope this increases your circulation." She did not know it, but she had only one year left to live.

Today, the director of the now defunct *France-Dimanche* still remembers Piaf as someone irreplaceable. "Charismatic" is the word he uses over and over again when talking about her. "Twice we published her memoirs," he notes, "and each time the circulation of the paper went up

188

by 300,000 copies! Who else could ever do that for a paper?" Then he talked about her lingering illness. "You know, from 1960 on people expected her to die, and the stories we ran about her over those last three years kept the paper alive during that time. Since Piaf, there's been nobody like her. Never will be. If she were alive today, could even she keep a paper like ours going? I doubt it. Television hurt us even back in those days. Today it would murder us. Television killed all the papers like ours."

So Piaf—with the blessing of her people—was going to marry Théo, at the Town Hall of Paris' Sixteenth *Arrondissement,* On October 9, 1962. An enormous crowd gathered at the Town Hall that day, mostly women, who drowned out with their cries of "Long live France's little fiancée" the few "You lousy pimp!" and "Gigolo!" that were aimed at young Théo, who would spend the next several years paying off Edith's enormous debts, before dying himself in an automobile accident seven years later.

The questions that Théo had to field from the journalists that day were insane, but they were not as bad as some of those he had to cope with later. Edith had to restrain him on more than one occasion.

"What use is love?"

"How does it feel to be marrying someone twenty years older than you?"

"Age isn't everything. Besides, Edith is a child in many ways."

"Do you expect to have children?"

"If my wife wants to."

But *France-Dimanche* took the cake with its two inimitable headlines:

EVEN IF MY FATHER REFUSES HIS CONSENT, EDITH,
I'LL STILL MARRY YOU

and:

WHEN THEO'S MOTHER, WHO IS ONLY EIGHT YEARS OLDER THAN ME
SAID TO ME, "EDITH, CALL ME 'MOTHER,'" IT WAS MORE THAN I
COULD BEAR. I BROKE DOWN AND SOBBED.

If Edith's honeymoon with Jacques Pills was spent in a taxicab between two nightclubs in New York, her honeymoon with Théo would
take place in a detoxification clinic.

Later, Piaf mothered Théo: she would in fact make a singer out of
him, but she would soar to new heights when it came to dominating his
life. She was literally at the end of her strength. Théo rented a sumptuous
villa for her at Cap Ferrat, on the Riviera, complete with a large swimming pool. Edith forbade Théo to use it: she was afraid he might drown.
She also decided to teach him proper manners, and if he arrived five
minutes late for any meal, she would not let him eat. She only had
1,500,000 red corpuscles left, but she was still as authoritarian as ever.
Just like in the good old days.

In those good old days, she had always ordered for everyone in her
group. If she felt like having herring, everyone had herring. If she wanted
steak au poivre, it was steaks au poivre all around. But there were days
when she wasn't feeling up to snuff and when boiled rice was the menu,
in which case everyone had boiled rice or whatever else Edith's culinary
whim called for. In Edith's kingdom, she was queen, and no one had the
right to protest. She had an answer for everything. So what if she had one
foot in the grave? That didn't mean she didn't know what was good for
them. In this way she took her revenge for a thousand little slights she
had suffered in the past, from the time she had gone to sing for some
wealthy people and been made to go round back and come in through
the service entrance, to the time she had first been presented with a finger
bowl and, rather than dipping her fingers daintily in it, had picked it up
and downed the contents in one gulp. She would never forget the looks
on the faces of the guests that night!

She was Pygmalion and a born teacher, one who had to teach others
what she had learned through hard experience. Money? The least of her
concerns. With her it was easy come, easy go, and she never worried
about it: she could always get more if she needed it.

Most of all, perhaps, during that last year she was worried about Théo:
what would become of him in that show-business jungle after she was
gone? He wasn't as tough as she was, by a long shot. In the late summer
of 1963 he won a part in Georges Franju's film *Judex,* and she was happy
to see him leave for Paris, to move away from her coat-tails. If the truth
were known, however—and it is here that one gets a sense of the gran-
diose nature of the lady—she had probably begun to grow a little bored
with her young husband.

(*Opposite*) Théo and Edith
at their Cap Ferrat villa.

193

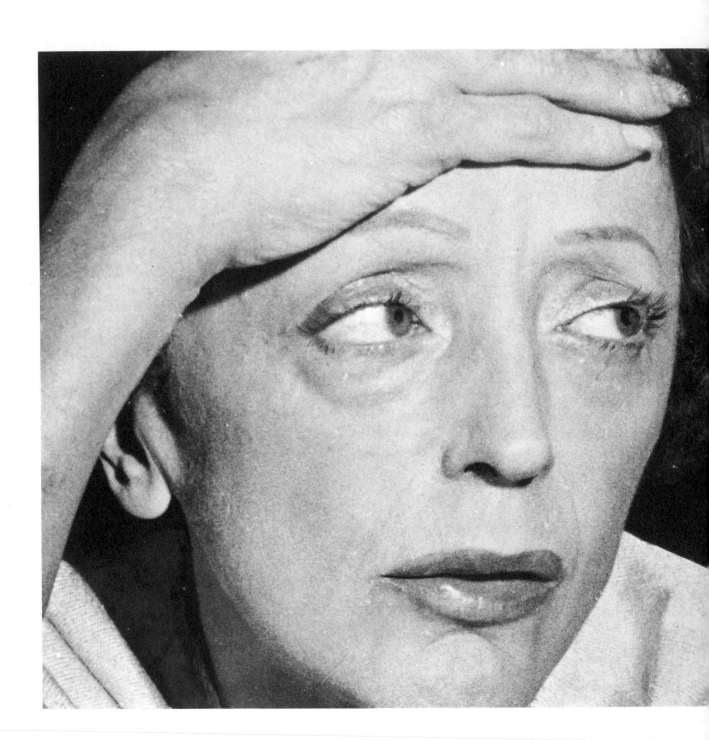

21

VULTURES AROUND PIAF

To her nurse, Simone
Margantin: "You'll see, after
I'm dead I'll come back and
pinch your feet."

—Edith Piaf

P iaf's last years remind one of a boxing match, and especially the kind of match that Montand sang about in *Battling Joe.* It's in the late rounds, and the face is cut and disfigured, the body hardly able to respond as once, twice, several times it hits the canvas only to pull itself up and mutter, to those who would like to stop the bout:

"Please. Don't stop it. I'll die if I can't fight. That's all I have left in the world!"

Piaf had come full circle: the end of her life was like the beginning, filled with pain and sorrow. She may well have been taken to various expensive hospitals and clinics for recovery, but it was the same little wounded bird, fallen out of its Ménilmontant nest, who lay there under the covers, each time making some chaotic effort to rise from her self-made ashes and go on living.

She who always wanted to be seen—on stage and in the press, for she hated it when people stared or pointed at her in public places, such as restaurants—was going to be ogled as she had never been, from her first days as a street singer in Pigalle.

"If you stop me from singing, I'll kill myself!"

Her dream was probably to die on stage, her last words an ultimate cry for love.

People in show business thought she was all washed up. She would show them. Jesus knew; so did Sister Theresa; and so did the people—the real people—of Paris. She would arise from her grave like Lazarus. Every time she managed to go on stage and give another performance, she knelt down afterward and thanked God. But there were times, too, when she simply collapsed: in Maubeuge and Belgium, she forgot her lines; in Dreux she simply could not go on. Her body was a welter of pain: her

ankles and her wrists especially made every day a living misery. It was a far cry from the days when she thought up ways of hiding what she considered her physical shortcomings by extraordinary movements or gestures, such as those of the clown in Lenoble's *Ballade du pauvre pendu.* It was a far cry from the days when, on first hearing a new song that had been presented to her, she would turn it down if she could not envision the gestures that she felt should accompany it. Now she was a prisoner of her own failing body, and its victim as well. There was, of course, still one recourse: drugs.

The journalists were pitiless in their probing, trying to make her confess that she knew she was about to die.

"Miss Piaf. As you may be aware, we keep hearing terrible stories about you, about your state of health, how poor it is, and that you're well aware of it, that this tour is a kind of suicide. Could you tell us what happened to you in Maubeuge?"

Edith remained unruffled. She had had the flu, she explained, so there was nothing so unusual about her having a fit of coughing before her first song. "It happens to everyone," she added, "singers especially."

"And so you had to stop singing?"

"Of course I did, since I couldn't sing and cough at the same time."

"If your doctor ordered you to stop singing, would you disobey him?"

The little girl from Pigalle, to whom Leplée had shouted one day after she had sneaked out of Gernys and gone back after a performance to sing in the street, "You're going to fall right back into the gutter," responded: "All I do is disobey. All I've done all my life is disobey."

A year later in Dieppe:

"Are you aware, Miss Piaf, that there's a rumor emanating from Paris that you died? Do you care to comment on that rumor?"

"That fact is, I wanted to see how far I could push myself, and I was wrong. But that's the way I've always lived: I'm only interested in going all the way."

"Are you afraid of dying?"

"No, I'm not afraid. . . . Just so long as I can sing . . ."

"You can't sing forever."

"I don't want to die an old lady."

199

22
THE PUBLIC PIAF

I wouldn't mind at all coming back to earth after my death.   —Edith Piaf

I'm sure that I've already been dead.
    —Edith Piaf, quoted in
    France-Dimanche

An opening night at the Olympia. In the front row are Alain Delon, Romy Schneider, Jean-Claude Brialy, and Jean-Paul Belmondo.

Piaf made Charlie Chaplin cry, as she did prostitutes and politicians, soldiers and sailors and aviators, mothers and homosexuals, tough boxers and jocks, poets and cops. She made the world cry. She was, in the true sense, a popular singer, of and for the people. The term fits her as well as did the little black dress that Leplée made her wear.

When filmmaker Alain Resnais asked Marguerite Duras to write the text of *Hiroshima mon amour* for him, he said to her: "I would like this film to resemble a song by Edith Piaf."

She probably never knew that, yet *Hiroshima mon amour* was one of her favorite films, and she used to go see it over and over again. That was the way she was when she loved something. She took her pals, her be-

When Alain Resnais asked Marguerite Duras to write the scenario for the film he was then planning, *Hiroshima mon amour,* he said: "I'd like this film to be like a Piaf song."

(Following double-page spread) Edith directing Felix Marten during a rehearsal at the Olympia.

Edith in 1960. Behind her is George Wilson; to her left, Jean Vilar, a leading director and producer, founder of the *Théatre National Populaire*.

Another Piaf first night, February 7, 1958. Among the first-nighters: publisher Guy Schoeller and his wife, the novelist Françoise Sagan.

Edith on June 11, 1952, at the height of her career and glory. She had just been awarded, by the Honorable Edouard Herriot, a member of the French Parliament, the prize of the *Académie du Disque*. On the left, the legendary Colette.

wildered little band, to see Monicelli's *Pigeon* no less than eight times, Ionesco's *The Chairs* eleven, Brecht's *Arturo Ui* six times, and the film *The Third Man* twenty evenings in a row. Near the end of her life, she used to read to them aloud from the works of the French theologian Teilhard de Chardin. Piaf-the-Tyrant was afraid to be alone, and she had an insatiable thirst to learn. Her intelligence was boundless, and all of it went into her work, from the earliest days to the last.

It is extraordinarily moving to listen to her records in chronological order. Try it some time, listening first to her earliest records and then skipping to the last—those she made just a few days before her death. The progress made by this grandchild of a Moroccan from Kabylia—a detail she carefully concealed from her French public in 1936, while she was openly proud of her drunken father, going so far as to take him with her on some of her early tours, when he was often mistaken for a porter or doorman, for he would never stay in swanky places with her, and would never remove his hat when he ate—the progress made by this astonishing voice is nothing less than remarkable.

Piaf knew her own limits, as well as she knew how to play on the public's naïveté. She used to cue her orchestra conductor to her evening's repertoire in this way: "First number I have down pat, it'll go fine. Two, three, four and five are O.K., so you don't have to worry about them. Number six I'm not so sure of, maybe I'll switch it at the last minute, so be on the lookout. No problem with any of the others, but let's make a special effort on the last three, to leave them high. I'll really go all out on those. And after it's all over we'll go out and have a drink together!"

Opening nights were when she really gave her all from beginning to end. She wanted to set the first-nighters on their ear. Thereafter the recitals could be uneven, or at least on a slightly lower plane, especially the second night, perhaps because of her post opening-night celebration. But she never disdained her public or took it for granted. She wanted to conquer it, win it over. "It was on stage that she really came alive," one of her ex-lovers commented, "it was during her performances that everything she had to give came out." But she didn't simply want to "give";

she wanted the public to share, to suffer with her, to live her lost loves and partake of her sorrow. She was Our Lady of Love, but also Our Lady of Masochists and even Our Lady of the Homosexuals. She left the subjects of motherhood, romance and happiness to others. After all, she didn't have much experience in that area. Not that she didn't sing of happiness, but when she did the audience knew it was fleeting, soon to be taken from her. Therein lay her major deceit. Ultimately she was cruel and spiteful, yet her supreme weapon was to make her public cry.

Edith was, in the final analysis, afraid of crowds, and of the emotions she knew she could provoke in an audience. She knew that with a single gesture, or intonation, she could have the world at her feet, but the power of that gesture transcended her sometimes. There was also the way she would pronounce the names of certain cities—Venice, Hamburg, Valparaiso—as though she knew them intimately as no one else could. The truth was, whenever she traveled she spent her time in any foreign city either on stage rehearsing or performing, or back in her room. Whether she went to America or Egypt, Sweden or Lebanon, she never "saw" where she was, never made any effort to get acquainted with the foreign cities. When she traveled she would either be knitting or partying. She took us to countries where we had never dreamed of going.

What she could do, as few others could, was to tear you away from your own life, out of yourself, and whisk you to the land where dreams come true. She could make soldiers win their battles, give virtuous women the lovers they had always longed for; she could make the poor forget their misery and the wealthy their boredom.

And having done all this, having reached a state of exaltation, she would fall, long and hard. After having shed seventeen songs, songs of love and despair and death, she found herself alone again. Alone as an animal is alone, and therein lies the explanation not only of her fears, but also of her cruelty and, ultimately, her downfall.

She sang so that other people could be torn asunder as she was. She sang to make people suffer as she had suffered, to rend their hearts, to tear them to shreds.

My heart is at the corner of a street
And often rolls into the gutter.
Dogs dashing after it, fighting,
The dogs are men, wolves.
My heart is already their fodder,
Nothing they do will disgust me.
Dear God, let not your creature
Suffer any more. Please take her.[16]

Yet she didn't want to die. But, in a final display of unrestrained exhibitionism, she showed herself broken down, in order to drive that image into the hearts of her public like a poisoned arrow.

"What I loved most about
her was her total sincer-
ity." Johnny Hallyday.

23
PIAF AND LOVE

Only budding love really
interested her. . . .
Afterwards, the path was
always the same.
— Charles Kiefer

None of us could ever give
her advice or help or defend
her unless there was the aura
of love in the background. To
become a friend, all you had
to do was change the dream.
— Henri Contet

She was Fate, the instrument
of Destiny, a man-eater.
— Pierre Hiégel

I don't even think she had
deep relations with them.
She came. She went. Lots of
hustle and bustle. But most
of it was in her head.
— Billy

E dith's life can be told in much the same way as the history of art. The way one speaks of the Neo-Classical period, or the Impressionist period, or Cubist period, so with Piaf one can, realistically, break her life down into sections dominated by those she was involved with: the Asso period, the Meurisse period, the Montand period, the Cerdan period, and so on. And these are only the "stars." There were many others.

The average length of these "periods," according to the testimony of Andrée Bigard, who lived as close to her as anyone for more than ten years, was about two years. From all reports it was not the physical side of love that drew her to her lovers so much as the state of being in love.

218

The notion. She loved looking deep into their eyes as she told them the story of her life.

She wearied quickly of her lovers, whether it was some dumb member of the male chorus behind her humming or repeating her refrains, or one of her bicycle racers whose trial runs she would time in the Bois de Boulogne. No matter whom she chose, she was never afraid of ridicule, of what people would say about her man of the hour. She was above ridicule. The men whom her groupies referred to as the "New Boss" came and went through her messy apartment like so many fleeting meteors, or, more accurately, so many falling stars.

All her friends give proof. The minute she was smitten, everyone could

219

see it. And from that moment on, the then "Boss" was on his way out, though he may not yet have known it. Edith's inimitable combination of ferocity and bad faith would see to it. It was a pattern that marked her life from her earliest days. And when the old "Boss" had gone down in disgrace, woe unto any members of the inner circle who might take his defense. The Old Boss is dead! Long live the New! And no protests were tolerated.

Piaf thrived on drama. She loved to laugh, and she loved dramatic situations—most of which she created. She never sang as well or movingly as when she was in the throes of a crisis. Her most emotional performances took place when she had just broken off with a lover.

Or perhaps, as she herself confessed at one point, it was all an act, carefully orchestrated and suited to her needs of the moment. She had the same sort of relationships with her lovers as she did with her musicians and lyricists. She was capable of changing them from one day to the next, or renouncing them the moment she sensed that their songs were no longer right for her or failed to stimulate her any longer.

When it came to sensing what was right for her, her intuition was impeccable. Her musical instinct was infallible, and she tested it again and again in her work and before her public, a public she possessed in a way she had never possessed any man.

Her Pygmalionism when it came to love has already been mentioned, and is undoubtedly basic to her character. When she saw a man for the first time, and it "clicked," Edith's fantasy showed him on stage, not in bed. On this score, the case of Yves Montand is classic, for if she foresaw with blinding lucidity the scope and extent of his future as an artist, she was also quick to sense that he was someone to be feared. After having launched him with a generosity that has rarely been equaled, she did not hesitate to try and do him in with extraordinary cruelty as soon as she realized that he was threatening to become a dangerous rival.

Edith was an Arab sheik who played at being a woman.

She sang of men who had made her suffer, of the man waited for who never returns, but the truth was, in most cases it was she who discarded them. When confronted with that, Edith's response was that if she did it was because she was afraid of being left, and preferred to act first. It seems, however, that she dropped them because she was afraid they might soon begin to bore her.

Piaf was, in short, one of the most impatient creatures who ever lived, and it was this impatience that dictated her love life. A love life, one might add, that was always astride the twin extremes of vaudeville and tragedy.

24

GOD AND PIAF

"You see, I still thank Jesus for allowing me to sing." God was a word she didn't know.   —Simone Margantin

Perhaps Saint Theresa found that Edith was exaggerating a bit. She hadn't given her a new lease on life to fill the Olympia to the rafters, to stand the *tout Paris* on its ear, or to make headlines for fifteen years in *France-Dimanche*.   —Bernard Pivot

Like everything you do, you wanted to rush into meditation.

—Simone Margantin

All those who appreciated the talent of Edith Piaf are grieved by the news of her death. Christians aware of her great gifts of charity and her deep-rooted faith will need no prompting to pray for her soul and ask for divine mercy at Mass. Although the honors that the Church reserves for its departed cannot be offered her because of an irregular situation, the chaplain of the Catholic Union will come to the Père-Lachaise cemetery Monday morning to pray at the artist's grave.

—Communiqué of the
Archbishop upon
the death of Edith Piaf

One of the constants in Piaf's life, and one of her pillars of strength, was her faith. Her relations with God were intimate, although she was wont to be unfaithful to Him with Sister Theresa, who was always her favorite.

She mixed God into everything. He was always there. On stage. In her bed. In her finances.

"If God has allowed me to earn so much money," she used to say, "it is because He knows I give it all away."

It was always her feeling—as was true for Cerdan, and perhaps everyone who has known poverty—that the sums of money she was paid were excessive.

She was generous to a fault. On the first of each month her secretary would send checks to no fewer than fifteen people whom Edith had decided to help. These were not the members of the inner circle, the usual spongers, but people whom Edith never saw. She supported them, but she didn't want to see them. It was her way of being a Christian: blind charity.

Before she went on stage, she would always make the sign of the cross, and she prayed at least half an hour each day in her room, all alone.

But more than anything else, she mixed God into her private life. One gets a whiff of it in many of her songs;

> *Dear God, please let me keep him*
> *Just a little bit more*
> *This man I adore . . .*
> *Our love, which pleases Him*
> *Is purer than the driven snow*
> *That much I know . . .*[17]

When Piaf fell in love with a man who didn't want her to drink, she climbed the steep steps of Montmartre and made a vow in the Sacré-Coeur church not to have a drink for a year. When the man in question didn't last the full year, Piaf's accounting system with God was such that she would go to any lengths not to break her pact, however absurd.

Feeling responsible for Cerdan's death, since it was she who had asked him to move up his trip and take the fatal plane, she went to Mass every morning for several months. And when her American agent, Clifford Fischer, died, she dragged Andrée Bigard twice a week with her to the synagogue, to pray for him to whom she attributed her great American success.

When she was still young, still Kid Piaf barely off the streets, she used to murmur: "God, am I scared! I don't know why, but I'm terrified. I know something's going to happen to me. I don't know what, but I feel it will be something awful, something irreparable."

She believed in reincarnation. And she hated cemeteries. Toward the end of her life she became a Rosicrucian and spent considerable time every day meditating.

Piaf's intimate relationship with God and those around Him says a lot about her way of thinking. Only a few days before her death she confided to her nurse, "You know, I've been thinking about Jesus. Don't you find it a bit strange that, since He was living with His family and all, He up and left them just when they needed Him most?"

Edith Peals

CHATEAU MARMONT
8221 SUNSET BOULEVARD
HOLLYWOOD 46, CALIFORNIA
HOLLYWOOD 9-2911

Le 24 dec. 1952

Dieu bleu

Voici le chèque pour la fin de mois, j'ai doublé, Chang, Yvonne, Jolivet, Berg, garcia et vous, avertissez tous ce petit monde que c'est a l'occasion de la fin d'année pour leur éviter d'en prendre l'habitude chaque fin de mois ce que me serait fort désagréable!..

Extract from a letter written from Hollywood on Christmas Eve 1952, which gives a fair idea of why Edith never had any money. She encloses a check in her letter to Andrée Bigard, noting that "I'm doubling everyone's salary . . ." and adding, in a P.S.: "The cash left over is for you."

25
PIAF AND MONEY

In Sweden, while touring there, Edith suddenly had an overwhelming desire for a steak and French fries, some Camembert and red wine. What did she do? She rented a plane to take her and her musicians to Paris for lunch.
—*France-Soir*

Money? It didn't mean a thing to her. I've seen her slip several hundred francs to a beggar.   —André Pousse

Where did the money go? Into the bellies and pockets of her friends. At Edith's, everything was there for the asking—or even without asking. People went off with records, books, purses, phonographs, linen, even a coffee pot. Everything disappeared. Anyone, at any hour of the day or night, was free to raid the refrigerator or pantry. But what ruined her more than anything else was the army of "friends" who borrowed money from her and never paid it back. And Edith never asked for it—not once in her life.
—Jean Noli

Piaf's relationship with money is more than a trifle mad at all times, and utterly extravagent. It perfectly explained the extreme poverty of her youth, and the feeling that she had to work not only for herself but for others too: her father, the pimps, and finally for those who lived off her, whether they called themselves the inner circle or others called them spongers. Her comment about Jesus leaving home rather than working to help support His family says a lot about her feelings on this score.

230

As a child Piaf was familiar with both cold and hunger. Even if she denied it later, she did beg in the streets as a child. There she was with her hand out, asking passers-by for a coin to buy a crust of bread . . . and the next thing she knew she had more money than she knew what to do with. Rags to riches, all because of that great gift: her voice. She always used to say that she would still be on the streets if it weren't for her voice.

Go back to age seven: Edith, a scrawny little kid, was singing in the streets and the Paris courtyards, while Momone took up the collection.

"Ten of us would leave the theater, but by the time we arrived at the restaurant the party somehow had grown to forty."

231

With the money they raised, she used to buy food and drink for the other poor kids of Belleville, Ménilmontant and later Pigalle. The kids grew into men, and later when Edith fell in with some pretty tough company, some of them were always there to bail her out. They never forgot.

Maybe it was her fascination with the world of pimps, but Edith always had a strong tendency to let herself be "taken," even after she had become the Great Piaf. During World War II, when she was living at Madame Billy's on the rue de Villejust, she used to "lose" at least two alligator purses a week. The truth was, she sold them at half price to some girl friends, so that she could pay some pimp or gigolo she had had a one-night stand with, then cook up some wild story for her lover of the moment as to her whereabouts.

From the day she first realized that the voice she possessed was worth a mint, and that she could make a fortune just by opening her mouth, she made up her mind to give it away as fast as she made it. Everything. All around. But her generosity had other facets: it was also the means by which to buttress her desire to dominate.

All her lovers benefited from that generosity, and the pattern was always the same. First came the gold cigarette lighter from Cartier's; then the cuff-links, sometimes with diamonds; a gold signet ring; one, or several, dark blue suits. The suits were always a trifle too tight, the shoes a trifle too snug. Just to remind the gentlemen in question not to get too big for their britches.

During the war, Piaf was singing in a cabaret in Marseille. Andrée Bigard was with her, and it was she who took charge of all the finances, paying everything—room, meals, travel, gifts. It was a formal arrangement that Piaf had made between them. Each week Andrée gave Edith her pocket money—the equivalent of about 500 francs today. At the time, Edith was earning about five times that much each night: 300 francs if she were working only one cabaret, double that or more if she were working two.

One Wednesday Edith asked Bigard if she would mind advancing her the following week's allowance. Bigard refused, "unless you tell me what you want to use it for, Edith."

It was carnival time in Marseille. And Edith quite simply wanted to squander her next week's allowance on a young soldier she had met . . . But she had no intention of admitting that to Bigard.

Blind with rage, Edith simply said: "O.K. I'll make you pay for that!"

That night, after the show, they went out to dinner with Michel Emer, who was hiding out in Marseille from the Nazis, and whom Edith was helping support.

As was the case each time that Edith entered a restaurant, the people there recognized her and applauded her—something that made her se-

cretly happy but also truly embarrassed her. Now, before she was served, Edith got to her feet and addressed the customers:

"Ladies and gentlemen. First of all, thank you for your kind applause. As you know, I've just finished my stint at the cabaret, and it's quite late. Yet my secretary, this lady sitting right here beside me, refuses to give me any money. Tell me what you'd like to hear me sing. I'll sing whatever you like, after which I'll take up a collection, if you don't mind."

Bigard was horribly embarrassed. "Edith, what in the world are you doing? And besides, you'll get into trouble with the cabaret. You've got a contract not to sing anywhere else!"

"I couldn't care less!"

She sang, to prolonged applause, and Michel Emer took up the collection. The cabaret made no trouble.

Another night Michel Emer, wanting to show his gratitude to Edith, invited her to a black-market restaurant in Marseille. The owner greeted them with a crestfallen air. "I'm so sorry," she said, "this is not your night. I'm fresh out of all my normal delicacies. All I have is fennel and cream cheese tonight."

"Well, Michel," said Piaf with a laugh, "so this is your three-star restaurant, is it? Congratulations!"

Several days later Emer discovered the truth. It was a Piaf set-up: she had called the owner that afternoon and asked her to go along with her

little game. She knew Emer could not afford the evening he had planned, and wanted to keep the man who had just written for her the song *D'l'autre côté de la rue* from wasting his money.

Piaf, obsessed by the memory of her mother's wretched and miserable death, took it upon herself to take care of a whole swarm of elderly people. She was forever slipping them a hundred franc note.

"Thank you, Madame Piaf! I was afraid you'd gone away on a trip."

"Don't worry, my friend, I stayed to make sure I didn't miss you."

From San Francisco, Edith called her personal physician to ask him to take care of the old lady who sold her newspapers on the corner. "Listen, doctor, she's very sick. Please make sure she has a private room. And give her whatever she needs. I'll see you're reimbursed as soon as I get back to Paris."

It turned out that the little old lady had been put into a ward, and according to the doctor had only a few hours to live.

"I seem to remember she always wanted to be cremated. Can you take care of that, doctor?"

The undertaker asked the doctor whether or not the old lady had a burial vault. The doctor passed on the question to San Francisco.

"No, of course she doesn't. Will you buy one for her? I'll pay for it."

After the Liberation of Paris in 1944, when Andrée Bigard left, Lou Barrier took over and managed Edith's affairs. At this stage of her career Edith was earning more and living on a higher level. The less she knew about her household budget the better she liked it.

As for her professional life, however, it was quite the contrary. She knew exactly what each of her musicians was earning, and she never forgot to leave a special tip for the stage hands wherever she sang. There were even times when she had the flu and was running a high fever but still went on, not so much for her public as for the usherettes, who she knew would be laid off if she called off the performance.

When Bruno Coquatrix was facing bankruptcy, Edith did not hesitate, despite her precarious health, to throw herself into the fray in a valiant effort to save the Olympia Theater.

There is a curious money-bond between Piaf and her public. The people who came to hear her loved to remember that Piaf had once been poor, had come from the lower depths, from the people, and they reveled in the thought that with that voice, straight out of the gutter, she earned millions. A strange bond between those two, Piaf and her public: she was blazing, and they wanted to see her rich, bruised, and loved!

The headlines of *France-Dimanche* are eloquent:

I THREW A MILLION FRANCS OUT THE WINDOW

IN NEW YORK, THEY PAID ME THOUSANDS OF DOLLARS A NIGHT

IN MY HOUSE IN BOULOGNE, I HAVE A STAFF OF EIGHT

FROM MY RECORDS ALONE, I EARN MILLIONS OF FRANCS YEARLY

Piaf ran into Aznavour, where he and a fellow singer named Roche had a two-man act. Aznavour came from the same lower depths as Piaf.

She lived well, with often a chauffeur and expensive car, but most of her money went to others, or straight out the window.

237

His were from Armenia. She convinced him he was wasting his time with the duo act, and made him quit. To do what? To become her slave. "I did everything," Aznavour relates. "I kept her records, balanced her budget, I checked out her lighting and made sure her microphones were working, and the curtains too. I even served as her chauffeur. I was her gentleman companion." He too recognized how much alike they were.

"He's kind of cute, your boyfriend," a female friend of Piaf's confided to her. "Why don't you get him to shorten his nose?"

"She's right, you know," Piaf said.

"Absolutely!" Eddie Constantine agreed.

Piaf was as happy as a lark. They were going to trim Charles' nose! What an excellent idea: she would give him a new nose, and at the same time celebrate the demise of the old one. After several glasses of wine, she burst out laughing.

"You know, Charles, there's only one problem. Your whole personality is in your nose."

"Then let's not trim it," Charles suggested.

"Impossible! I've already paid a deposit on it."

238

Later, when Piaf was ruined and deeply in debt, she was still grist for the *France-Dimanche* mill:

PIAF LAMENTS: NOW AZNAVOUR IS RICHER THAN I AM!

When she fell ill in Stockholm, after she had collapsed on stage, an intestinal occlusion was diagnosed. The king's surgeon was scheduled to operate. Piaf-the-Whimsical decided she'd rather go back to Paris. The next plane was not scheduled to leave for several hours. The next day the newspapers blared:

'I RENTED A DC4 ALL FOR ME.'

She was so weak she could barely stand up when she went back on stage to pay for that DC4, but that was part of her character: she had to wow her public, no matter what the cost or pain to herself . . . she didn't know any other way.

Edith used to receive weekly reports on the sale of her records, and whenever she would catch one or the other of her fleeting lovers noting down in a little notebook the impressive numbers, it always made her laugh. The singer Felix Marten (who noted, "When first we met I was singing about cynicism and women; Edith wanted me to sing about love, but I wasn't old enough for that") used to amuse Edith because he couldn't bear the way she threw her money around. "She used to slip me money to pay for all sorts of bills," he said. "It used to make me sick every time. At the restaurant, as many as forty people would often show up for a late-night dinner. And guess who always picked up the check? If ever I dared say anything to her she'd give me a withering look and say: 'What the hell do you care? It's not your money!' The fact was, many's the night I remember our leaving the theater with, say, about ten or a dozen people in our crowd, and by the time we reached the restaurant there were thirty-five or forty."

"Edith," grumbled Lou Barrier, "if you keep this up, you'll soon find yourself back at the Ambassadeurs Theater, not on stage but as an usherette!"

"Have you forgotten that you're talking to Edith Piaf!" she said imperiously—the Kid from Belleville . . . and Gernys and Marseille and New York.

"You could never get the last word with her," Billy sighed. "There was something about her, something *in* her that prevented anyone from scolding or admonishing her. Even when she was drunk she was still Queen Piaf."

"Money?" Edith used to say. "How did I lose it? I never did *lose* it. I just never knew where it went."

"Now Aznavour has more money than I do!"

26
BRIC-A-BRAC

Madame, no one since Sarah Bernhard has the movements and poses on stage that you have.   —Charles Dullin

Since Edith Piaf's death, life to me seems insipid.
                —Simone Margantin

Poets always pretend they're asleep. But they're not.
                —Jean Cocteau

It's not her fault if she radiates misery, if we picture her better in a hospital bed than in quilted satin, if she bears all the stigmata of unhappiness. She does her best to escape the dark shadows that surround her. She buys her clothes at Jacques Fath's. She wears mink. She goes to the hairdresser. She lives in the Bois de Boulogne. She has a Chinese cook, and reads Homer. But the mink looks like rabbit on her, and the curls spill around her face like those of a lost little boy. . . . The swanky home takes on an air of some hastily furnished stage set which will disappear at a sign from the stagehand. The Chinese cook looks like a walk-on, and Homer teaches her simply that, nine centuries before Christ, poets were already singing of suffering. The way she does. . . . All she has left to break the terrible silence of her heart is the sound of her public applauding.
                —Françoise Giroud,
                France-Dimanche

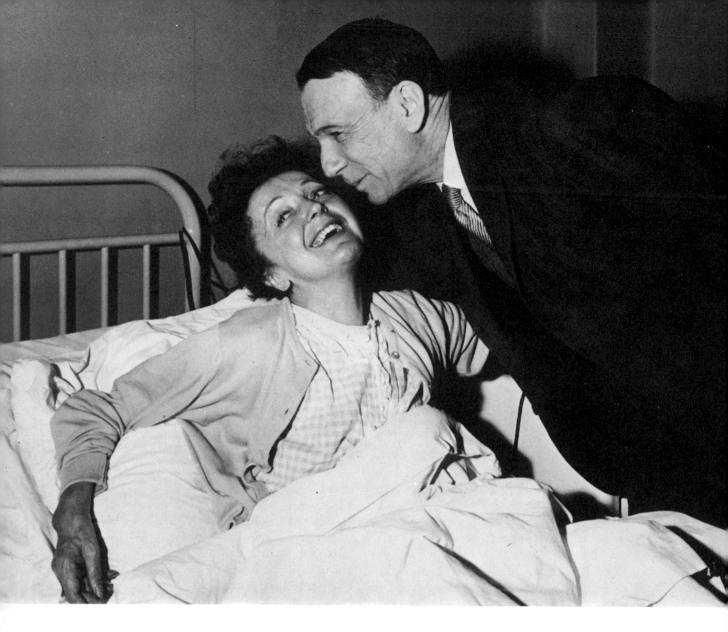

Edith and Henri Contet at the American Hospital in Paris. "She was capable of incredible acts of kindness and generosity. . . ."

Now we must rush pell-mell through all sorts of random notes and thoughts gathered while researching and writing this book, notations that have a bearing on who and what Piaf was that have not found their way into the text. Like stuffing the Christmas stocking for all those Christmases she never had. In no special order, then:

Her disorder . . . The sweaters she was forever knitting for her lovers, none of which she ever finished . . . The furniture in her apartment, which looked as though some absent-minded mover had just set it down, any which way (the only time in her life she had any decent furniture was when she invited the film actress Michèle Morgan to her apartment . . . and for that occasion she rented it!) . . . The appointments she made for five o'clock, with half a dozen people (or more) at the same time . . . Her voice, sharp like a snapping flag in the wind when she gave an order . . . Her fear—no, downright terror—of eating in restaurants, not to men-

tion dining cars and hospitals . . . Her fear of flying . . . Her passion for astrology (whenever a prospective lover's sign was incompatible with hers—Sagittarius—she would work on it till she had solved the problem) . . . The words she uttered most often in her songs: black, blue, boy, caress, cry, despair, death, drunk, fate, goodbye, happy, heart, hell, hurt, light, lost, love, lover, man, over, sailor, shame, sky, sorrow, tears . . . The verbal limitations of her repertoire led the Duke de Brissac to remark, somewhat acidly: "There are 250,000 words in the French language. What a pity that this recital makes use of no more than 150!" . . . Her childish side: she had kept till the end of her life Cerdan's boxing gloves and his robe . . . Her need to laugh, so compulsive that it sometimes led her to acts of real cruelty.

"Yet she could be meek and gentle as a lamb," noted Henri Contet, "and spend a whole afternoon caressing your cheek. But," he was quick to add, "she was also capable of locking you in your room until you came

She had traveled everywhere, from the U.S. to Egypt, from Sweden to Lebanon. But she never really *saw* any of the places she visited.

243

up with a song she liked. 'I'm not letting you out till you come up with something great! Think about me, it'll inspire you to write. And remember: Shakespeare was an amateur compared to you!' " However one may question the methods, the fact remains that she managed to "extract" several marvelous songs in this way: *Bravo pour le clown; Regarde-moi toujours comme ça; Padam, padam; T'es beau, tu sais.* Contet, who experienced the emotional "terrorism" of Edith's passion, confessed that there was nothing more moving than to watch Piaf backstage, her eyes fixed on the man singing on stage. "You could *see* the love brimming out of those eyes," he said, "even if you knew that she was seeing the man who would replace you in her affections, it was still extraordinary." In this instance, the man she was watching was the young Yves Montand.

Piaf was painfully aware of her physical shortcomings, especially when she was young, and was profoundly hurt by some of the adjectives strewn throughout the early reviews: "scrawny," "skinny," "sickly," "rachitic." But the real pain came later, in the days when the crowd was on its feet, applauding, while she was literally burning up. Like most artists she never felt the pain while she was singing, but after it was over it was more than she could bear. And generally the applause lasted for several minutes. In Holland, in 1962, for over ten minutes. In her 1961 recital at the Olympia—which was recorded and became one of her best-selling records—the applause would have filled one whole side of the record if it had not been cut.

Charismatic: she exuded a magnetism, a flow, that everyone around her could feel.

I could go on and on . . . for I find it as hard to leave her as her audience did at the end of her concerts.

At the end of each recital, she always said "thank you" to her public.

Piaf in Egypt, astride a camel whose name was Mistinguett!

27
IMMORTALITY

For me, sleeping is a waste
of time. I'm afraid to sleep.
It's a kind of death. I hate
sleep.   —Edith Piaf

The crowds at Père-La-chaise cemetery in Paris the day of Piaf's burial. Marlene, beautiful as ever, strides through the throng.

Piaf's funeral, on October 14, 1963, had all the pomp and circumstance of a state funeral. The crowds were enormous, and they were moved to tears. Many cried, some sobbed, and others screamed to the Little Sparrow they had lost. "Sleep in peace, my brave little Piaf," read the legend on Maurice Chevalier's wreath. One sensed that the crowd didn't really believe she was gone, that the voice was really stilled; it somehow fully expected that she would miraculously emerge from her coffin and break into one of her favorite songs: *J'm'en fous pas màl; Allez, venez Milord;* or *Les Mômes de la cloche.* And if that miracle were not to occur, then it would be consoled to some extent at the sight of Marlene's or Aznavour's tears, or Charles Dumont's stricken face, or that of the young husband Théo.

248

Sur les marches de cette maison
naquit le 19 Décembre 1915
dans le plus grand dénuement
EDITH PIAF
dont la voix, plus tard,
devait bouleverser le monde

(Above) Commemorative plaque placed on the wall of the house where Edith was born. The ceremony designating the house a landmark, which took place on November 8, 1966, roughly three years after her death, drew a huge crowd (top, opposite).

Piaf had always said: "I bet there'll be a huge crowd at my funeral." It was one of the biggest understatements of the day. "The pity is she's not here to see it," said her favorite photographer Hugues Vassal, "one of her biggest triumphs."

In the Soviet Union, where she had never set foot, the Russian artists observed a minute of silence when her death was announced. Robin Smith, writing in America just before her death, poignantly noted: "Edith Piaf, France's best loved singing star, is singing herself to death and won't allow anyone to stop her."

Just a year before her death, for the gala celebration of the opening of the film *The Longest Day,* she had agreed to sing from the top of the Eiffel Tower. That night it was the writer Joseph Kessel who introduced her. Kessel was among those present the first night Edith sang at Leplée's. The circle was finally closed. Here are Kessel's words that night:

> There is no way to avoid the ineluctable signs of fate. I discovered Edith Piaf when she sang for the first time—and I mean the very first night—in a nightclub, a tiny creature in the midst of tables covered with bottles of champagne and people dressed to the teeth. She came directly from the street, from the pavement. Her ravaged face and the ragged sweater she was wearing that night bore eloquent testimony to the suffering of her childhood as clearly as any stigmata, and her voice was already filled with the unique genius that moved us so in the following years. And here she is tonight, on this enormous platform overlooking the entire city filled with bursting stars, over which her voice will soar like some magic bird. Even if this were not the Eiffel Tower, the heights she reached are enough to make one giddy, and yet in her there is nothing immoderate or undeserving. Everything artificial is alien to her, as is trickery and fleeting fashion. One cannot even ascribe her rise to fame in any way to luck. She earned her fame, step by painful step. To scale these heights, Edith has paid the price and paid it dearly: poverty overcome, weakness and anguish mastered, artistic standards of the highest order, and an incredible courage.

(Below, opposite) The tens of thousands waiting in line for hours, on the Boulevard Lannes, to catch a glimpse of the singer the day before her burial.

Ironically, the French poet and Edith's friend, Jean Cocteau, died the same day. His fame too was great, but the crowds at his funeral were

small compared to hers. Both would have enjoyed not only the shared date but the comparative statistics at their final rites.

Then both entered the realm of legend. Piaf, like Cocteau, would soon appear in the new editions of the French encyclopedias. And that would have pleased her too, for it was the extent of her ignorance that bothered her, and often accounted for the cruelty of which she has been accused.

Only now could this fiery and impassioned little woman, whose relationship with music as with men was total and unremitting, finally sleep in peace, she who in life had disdained the world of dreams and was never able to fall asleep till dawn.

After his death, Théo Sarapo was buried next to Edith at Père-Lachaise. Each year, on All Saints Day, thousands still come to visit their graves.

SONGS IN FRENCH

1. From *Mon amant de la Coloniale*, 1936.
Words by Raymond Asso, music by
Juel. Les Editions de Paris, S.E.M.I.
Reprinted by permission.

Il avait en partant du front
Et descendant jusqu'au menton
Une cicatrice en diagonale,
Des cheveux noirs, des yeux tout pâles,
La peau brûlée par le soleil . . .

2. From *Les Hiboux*, 1935. P. Dalbret,
Joullot. Editions universelles.

Des gens rupins, des blasés, des vicieux,
avec leurs poules qui nous font les doux yeux,
viennent dans nos bouges
boire du vin rouge.
. . . On sent leur chair qui frémit dans nos bras,
alors on serre en leur disant tout bas:
c'est nous qui sommes les Hiboux, les apaches,
les voyous . . .

3. From *Mon coeur est au coin d'une rue*,
1937. A. Lasry, H. Coste. Editions
Lasry.

Hélas un soir, quelle tristesse,
Mon amant n'est pas revenu . . .

4. *Comme un moineau*, 1929. Words by
Marc Hély, music by Jean Lenoir.
Nouvelles Editions Méridian, Paris.

Le bec ouvert comme un moineau
L'oeil effronté comme un moineau
Chanter l'amour comme deux moineaux.

5. From *C'est d'la faute à ses yeux*, 1950.
Words and music by Edith Piaf. Or-
chestration by Robert Chauvigny. Editions Paul Beuscher.

J'avais tant d'amour pour un homme.
Il en avait si peu pour moi.
C'est peu de chose la vie en somme.
Je l'ai tué. Tant pis pour moi.

6. From *Mon Légionnaire*, 1936. Words
by Raymond Asso. Music by Marguerite Monnot. S.E.M.I., Paris.

Il avait de grands yeux très clairs
Où parfois passaient des éclairs
Comme au ciel passent les orages.
Il était plein de tatouages
Que j'ai jamais très bien compris.
Son cou portait "Pas vu, pas pris"
Sur son coeur, on lisait "Personne"
Sur son bras droit un mot "Raisonne."

7. *J'sais pas son nom,*
Je n'sais rien de lui
Il m'a aimée toute la nuit
Mon Légionnaire . . .

8. From *Les mots d'amour*, 1960. Words
by Michel Rivgauche, music by
Charles Dumont. Nouvelles Editions
Méridian, Paris.

Si un jour tu partais
Partais et me quittais
Me quittais pour toujours
Pour sûr que j'en mourrais
Que j'en mourrais d'amour.

9. From *Elle fréquentait la rue Pigalle,*
   1939. Words by Raymond Asso, music
   by Louis Maitrier. Editions Musicales
   Paul Beuscher, Paris.

   Elle fréquentait la rue Pigalle
   Elle sentait l'vice à bon marché
   Elle était tout' noire de péchés
   Avec un pauvre visage tout pâle.

10. From *Il n'est pas distingué,* 1936. P.
    Maye, M. Hély. Editions Salabert,
    Paris.

    Moi, Hitler, j'l ai dans l'blair. . . .
    Et je peux pas l'renifler
    les nazis ont l'air d'oublier
    qu'c'est nous dans la bagarre qu'on les
       a zioguillés.

11. Song written by Piaf for Yves Mon-
    tand, 1945.

    Elle a des yeux
    C'est merveilleux
    Et puis des mains
    Pour mes matins
    Elle a des rires
    Pour me séduire
    Et des chansons . . .
    Il y a elle
    Rien que pour moi
    Enfin . . . je le crois!

12. From *Le Droit d'aimer,* 1962. F. Lai, R.
    Nyel. Olympia.

    A la face des hommes
    Au mépris de leurs lois
    Jamais rien ni personne
    N'empêchera d'aimer.

13. From *La belle histoire d'amour,* 1961.
    Words by Edith Piaf, music by Charles
    Dumont. Les Nouvelles Editions Mé-
    ridian, Paris.

    Lorsq'un homme vient vers moi
    Je vais toujours vers lui
    Je vais vers j'n'sais quoi
    Je marche dans la nuit

14. From *C'est à Hambourg,* 1955. Words
    by Claude Delecluze and Michelle
    Senlis, music by Marguerite Monnot.

    Car moi j'suis comme la mer
    J'ai l'coeur trop grand pour un seul gars
    J'ai l'coeur trop grand et c'est pour ça
    Qu' j'écris l'amour sur toute la terre.

15. From *La belle histoire d'amour,* 1960.
    Words by Edith Piaf, music by Charles
    Dumont. Editions Méridian, Paris.

    Je cherche à t'oublier
    Et c'est plus fort que moi
    Je me fais déchirer
    Je n'appartiens qu'à toi.

16. From *Mon coeur est au coin d'une rue,*
    1937. A. Lasry, H. Coste. Courtesy
    Editions Lasry.

    Mon coeur est au coin d'une rue
    Et roule souvent à l'égout.
    Pour le broyer les chiens se ruent.
    Les chiens sont des hommes, des loups.
    Mon coeur est déjà leur pâture,
    Ma chair ne se révolte pas.
    Mon Dieu, que votre créature
    Ne souffre plus. Reprenez-la.

17. From *Mon Dieu,* 1960. Words by
    Michel Vaucaire, music by Charles
    Dumont. Courtesy Nouvelles Editions
    Méridian, Paris.

    Mon Dieu, laissez-le moi
    Encore un peu
    Mon amoureux . . .
    Notre amour fait plaisir à Dieu.
    Il est plus pur, il est plus clair
    Que l'eau limpide des rivières . . .

The Publishers wishes to thank the composers, lyricists and publishers, whose works have been quoted in this book.

Asso, Raymond
Chauvigny, Robert
Coste, H.
Dalbret, P.
Delecluze, Claude
Dumont, Charles
Editions Lasry
Editions Musicales Paul Beuscher
Editions Salabert
Editions universelles
Hely, M.
Henry Gilles
Joullot

Lai, F.
Lasry, A.
Lenoir, Jean
Maitrier, Louis
Maye, P.
Monnot, Marguerite
Nouvelles Editions Méridian
Nyel, R.
Olympia
Rivgauche, Michel
S. E. M. I.
Senlin, Michelle
Vaucaire, Michel

PHOTOGRAPH CREDITS